MW00679171

Deviance Among Physicians

The concept of deviance is complex, given that norms vary considerably across groups, times, and places. Society tends to primarily recognize traditional portraits of deviants such as street-offenders and drug addicts. The label "deviant" is commonly cast upon society's undesirables, but this socially constructed image often overlooks subtler—and arguably more dangerous—deviance. Physician malfeasance is an especially problematic form, given that medical professionals garner trust, autonomy, and prestige from society, which allows them to operate outside of the public eye.

This book responds to a growing number of concerns regarding deviant physician actions such as physically and sexually abusive behaviors, fabricating medical findings and records, and taking advantage of patients (e.g., filing fraudulent Medicaid claims). It explores theoretical explanations for physician deviance, and goes on to consider potential responses such as Medicaid Fraud Control Units, the *Questionable Doctors* database, and the ability of doctors to police themselves.

The unique perspective offered in this book informs discussions of white-collar crime and deviance and has important implications for researchers, policymakers, and students involved in criminal justice and public policy.

Thaddeus L. Johnson is a PhD Criminology & Criminal Justice candidate in the Andrew Young School of Policy Studies at Georgia State University in Atlanta, GA. An Andrew Young Fellowship recipient, he also serves as a graduate teaching assistant (GTA). Mr. Johnson's research interests include urban violence, police professionalism, and police behavior. His most recent work appears in the Criminal Justice Policy Review.

Natasha N. Johnson is a doctoral candidate in the Educational Policy Studies Department at Georgia State University in Atlanta, GA. Mrs. Johnson's research interests include educational justice/equity/equality, social justice leadership, curriculum development, and critical race and feminist theories. Her most recent work appears in Navigating Micro-Aggressions Toward

Women in Higher Education. In 2019, she was recognized as a University Council of Educational Administration (UCEA) David L. Clark Scholar.

Christina Policastro is a UC Foundation Assistant Professor of Criminal Justice in the Department of Social, Cultural, and Justice Studies at the University of Tennessee at Chattanooga. Her primary research interests are in the area of victimization with a specific focus on elder abuse and intimate partner violence. She has published articles on diverse topics, including perceptions of intimate partner violence victims, durable *medical equipment* fraud, pre-professionals' knowledge of elder abuse, and trajectories of recurring victimization among persons with serious mental illness. Her most recent work appears in *Journal of Quantitative Criminology*, *Journal of Interpersonal Violence*, and *Journal of Elder Abuse & Neglect*. In 2017, she received the New Scholar Award from the Academy of Criminal Justice Sciences' Division of Victimology.

Deviance Among Physicians
Fraud, Violence, and the Power to Prescribe

Thaddeus L. Johnson, Natasha N. Johnson, and Christina Policastro

Routledge
Taylor & Francis Group
NEW YORK AND LONDON

First published 2019
by Routledge
52 Vanderbilt Avenue, New York, NY 10017

and by Routledge
2 Park Square, Milton Park, Abingdon, Oxon, OX14 4RN

Routledge is an imprint of the Taylor & Francis Group, an informa business

© 2019 Taylor & Francis

The right of Thaddeus L. Johnson, Natasha N. Johnson and Christina Policastro to be identified as authors of this work has been asserted by them in accordance with sections 77 and 78 of the Copyright, Designs and Patents Act 1988.

All rights reserved. No part of this book may be reprinted or reproduced or utilised in any form or by any electronic, mechanical, or other means, now known or hereafter invented, including photocopying and recording, or in any information storage or retrieval system, without permission in writing from the publishers.

Trademark notice: Product or corporate names may be trademarks or registered trademarks, and are used only for identification and explanation without intent to infringe.

Library of Congress Cataloging-in-Publication Data
Names: Johnson, Thaddeus (Thaddeus L.) author.
Title: Deviance among physicians : fraud, violence, and the power to prescribe / Thaddeus Johnson, Natasha Johnson & Christina Policastro.
Description: Milton Park, Abingdon, Oxon ; New York, NY : Routledge, 2019. | Includes bibliographical references.
Identifiers: LCCN 2019008475 (print) | LCCN 2019010600 (ebook) | ISBN 9780429024474 (Ebook) | ISBN 9780367110505 (hardback) | ISBN 9780429024474 (ebk)
Subjects: LCSH: Physicians—Malpractice—United States. | Medical personnel—Malpractice—United States. | Medical ethics—United States.
Classification: LCC RA1056.5 (ebook) | LCC RA1056.5 .J64 2019 (print) | DDC 344.04/11—dc23
LC record available at https://lccn.loc.gov/2019008475

ISBN: 978-0-367-11050-5 (hbk)
ISBN: 978-0-429-02447-4 (ebk)

Typeset in Times New Roman
by Apex CoVantage, LLC

Contents

1 Introduction

The concept of deviance is complex, given that norms vary considerably across groups, times, and places. In our society, however, we tend to only recognize traditional portraits of deviants such as street-offenders and drug addicts. That is, the label deviant is commonly cast upon society's undesirables. But this socially constructed and widely accepted image often overlooks subtler, and arguably more dangerous malfeasance. A prime example of such non-conventional criminality is *physician deviance*—illicit or fraudulent acts committed by doctors (e.g., surgeons, dentists, psychiatrists, and so on) for personal gain within the context of their profession. This chapter provides an overview of key themes related to physician deviance including the concepts of trust and power, as well as situates the study of misconduct by medical professionals within its historical context and the broader white-collar crime literature. Finally, this chapter outlines the topics of discussion presented in the remaining chapters of the text.

During visits to our physician's office, hospital, or clinic, most of us would never imagine that the professionals we entrust both our lives and our family's lives with could be exploiting us. While most physicians adhere to the ethos, *primum non nocere*,[1] a sizable portion victimize the very individuals and systems they solemnly vowed to protect (Iglehart, 2009; Policastro & Payne, 2013). Medical practitioners are hardly the only professional group to prioritize profit and power over everything else (e.g., patient well-being). Unlike other occupations, however, persons within our society place inimitable levels of trust in the verity of health care professionals (Blendon, Benson, & Hero, 2014). More notably, the amount of faith we have in our physicians far surpasses that of other professionals within and external to the medical sector (Gidman, Ward, & McGregor, 2012). Think, for a moment, of doctors' inevitable presence in and throughout most of our lives. When we are born, a doctor is there. When we die, they are usually there during our final days. In other words, from our very first moments of existence, we are taught to trust doctors.

Because of physicians' privileged or "hero" status within our society (Arnulf & Gottschalk, 2013), they enjoy unparalleled public confidence and embedded expectations that cannot be understated (Cruess, 2006; Wynia, 2008). Evidence of widespread fidelity to doctors has been observed among the general public and academics alike. Edwin Sutherland (1949), for instance, who first coined the phrase "white-collar crime," connoted that physicians were far more honorable than other professionals and, thus, unlikely to engage in occupational deviance (Wilson, Lincoln, Chappell, & Fraser, 1986). Sutherland's stance was undoubtedly inaccurate but reflects the unmatched confidence society has long placed in these clinicians.

Unbeknownst to many, this honorable and highly trusted profession is replete with a myriad of illegal activities, ranging from medical insurance fraud to physical/sexual abuse (Payne, 2012). With their power and prestige, coupled with a highly specialized knowledge-base and skill-set, come great autonomy. Doctors mostly operate outside of the public's watchful eye in an environment teeming with opportunities for crime and deviance. Even though physicians are subject to sanctions from medical boards, the current landscape lends itself to a lack of oversight and repercussions for misbehavior. Take, for example, Grant and Alfred's (2007) evaluative piece on physician discipline, sanctions, and recidivism. Through this work, they found "a very large number of repeat offenders among physicians who have received board sanctions, indicating a possible need for greater monitoring of disciplined physicians or less reliance upon rehabilitative sanctions" (p. 867). Similar to other white-collar professionals, the skill, sophistication, resources, and influence of doctors afford them ample opportunity to evade detection, prosecution, and conviction (Benson, 2016).

Against this backdrop, it should come as no surprise that the power and authority granted to physicians have led to dramatic growth in the rates and forms of medical deviance throughout the last century. However, criminality and exploitation in medicine is not a contemporary problem. Nor is it unique to the United States. Stretching back nearly 2,500 years to the time of Hippocrates—medicine's preeminent historical figure—concerns about medical misconduct were evident with the creation of the "Hippocratic Oath" (Edelstein, 1943; Hulkower, 2016; Miles, 2005). The establishment of this longstanding convention would suggest that medicine's "dark side" has remained a chief public policy issue for over two millennia.

An expansive collection of literature and legal artifacts demonstrates that the immense power afforded to doctors has been a point of contention throughout human history. The Roman Empire's Constitutio Criminalis Carolina of 1592, for example, criminalized physician actions that led to the loss of patient life (Langbein, 1974). Roughly 100 years later, a controversial piece entitled *The Conclave of Physicians, Detecting their Intrigues,*

Frauds, and Plots Against their Patients (Harvey, 1686) highlighted misconduct among French doctors. Fast forwarding to the 20th century, Sir William Osler, "the father of modern medicine," pointed out what he believed to
be the root of all medical crime—isolation and arrogance. He notes:

> No class of men needs friction so much as physicians; no class gets
> less. The daily round of a busy practitioner tends to develop an egoism
> of a most intense kind, to which there is no antidote. The few setbacks
> are forgotten, the mistakes are often buried, and ten years of successful
> work tend to make a man touchy, dogmatic, intolerant of correction,
> and abominably self-centered.
>
> (Cushing, 1940, p. 447)

Interestingly, these themes also figure centrally in explanations of white-
collar offending. Characterized by deceit and violation of trust, illicit activities among physicians epitomize Sutherland's (1949) privileged crime
perspective. *White-collar crime*, according to Sutherland (1949), refers to
"illegal acts committed by a person of respectability and high social status
in the course of his occupation" (p. 9). Although this seminal definition
has undergone numerous iterations (see, Brightman, 2011; Edelhertz, 1983;
Robin, 1974; Strader, 2011), in its purest form, elite crimes describe profit-
driven offenses perpetrated by persons within positions of trust (e.g., doctors, politicians, attorneys). In some instances, those in power take advantage
of situations simply because they have the faculty to do so. Irrespective of
the motive, white-collar offenders, including physicians, exploit their high
status and wealth without regard for the law or their victims. Even more
disturbing is the fact that society's most vulnerable persons (e.g., mentally
ill and poor) usually bear the brunt of these crimes (Siegel, 2014).

Unfortunately, despite the prevalence and scope of physician deviance, it
has garnered remarkably little scholarly attention. Compared with our knowledge of street crime, the causes of elite medical crime are less well under-
stood. Numerous commentators contend that the unmatched trust, respect,
and authority doctors engender have contributed to a dearth of scholarship
on physician malfeasance (Pande & Maas, 2013). Whatever it is, the limited
scientific evidence makes it difficult to determine the full extent of this problem, and in turn, restricts our ability to identify actionable policy solutions.
Along with the public's steadfast faith in doctors, this paucity of literature has
helped mask illegitimacy within the profession (Morris, 2009).

Unfolding over five chapters, we take stock of and respond to a growing
number of concerns regarding unlawful physician actions. To better understand the issues surrounding this white-collar phenomenon, we explore various forms of physician deviance and crime, as well as potential criminological

explanations for and the current response(s) to misconduct among doctors. Within these areas, we include relevant, "real life" case examples of doctors misbehaving. More specifically, *Chapter 2* offers an extensive overview of different types of medical insurance fraud complete with estimates of the prevalence and economic impact of fraud. In this chapter, we draw upon routine activities theory (Cohen & Felson, 1979) and techniques of neutralization (Sykes & Matza, 1957) to account for the pervasiveness of fraud in the medical field. *Chapter 3* shifts focus to what we view as direct-contact, physically abusive behaviors committed by doctors including unnecessary medical surgeries/procedures and sexual misconduct. Detailed descriptions of the nature and extent of each form of physical abuse are presented. Control balance theory (Tittle, 1995, 2004) is applied to explain unnecessary medical procedures, while the rational choice framework (e.g., Clarke & Cornish, 2001; Cohen & Felson, 1979) is utilized to explain why a doctor may engage in sexually abusive behavior against a patient.

In light of recent, highly publicized scandals involving doctors (e.g., Larry Nassar) and the enormous costs of misconduct in the health care system, we also explore the variety of responses currently aimed at addressing this ongoing crime problem in *Chapter 4*. The fourth chapter highlights several key pieces of US legislation affecting health care professionals and enforcement efforts, as well as underscores key issues with the current response to fraud and abuse in the health care sector. Finally, drawing upon the criminological perspectives presented throughout the text, our closing chapter (*Chapter 5*) offers ideas for changes to the system and patient care that may minimize illicit conduct among society's elite medical professionals. Moreover, considering the scant literature dedicated to the topic of deviance by doctors, *Chapter 5* will also emphasize the need for future research in this area.

Note

1. *Primum non nocere* is a Latin phase meaning "first do no harm." As one of the foundational and universally respected principles among physicians, its primary consideration regarding treatment centers on the patient's well-being (Inman, 1861).

References

Arnulf, J. K., & Gottschalk, P. (2013). Heroic leaders as white-collar criminals: An empirical study. *Journal of Investigative Psychology and Offender Profiling*, *10*(1), 96–113.

Benson, M. L. (2016). Developmental perspective on white-collar criminality. In S. R. Van Slyke, M. L. Benson, & F. T. Cullen (Eds.), *The Oxford handbook of white-collar crime* (pp. 253–274). Oxford: Oxford University Press.

Blendon, R. J., Benson, J. M., & Hero, J. O. (2014). Public trust in physicians: US medicine in international perspective. *New England Journal of Medicine, 371*(17), 1570–1572.

Brightman, H. J. (2011). *Today's white collar crime: Legal, investigative, and theoretical perspectives*. New York: Routledge.

Clarke, R., & Cornish, D. (2001). Rational choice theory. In R. Paternoster & R. Bachman (Eds.), *Explaining criminals and crime* (pp. 23–42). Los Angeles: Roxbury.

Cohen, L. E., & Felson, M. (1979). Social change and crime rate trends: A routine activity approach. *American Sociological Review, 44*(4), 588–608.

Cruess, S. R. (2006). Professionalism and medicine's social contract with society. *Clinical Orthopaedics and Related Research, 449*, 170–176.

Cushing, H. (1940). *The life of Sir William Osler*. London: Oxford University Press.

Edelhertz, H. (1983). White-collar and professional crime: The challenge for the 1980s. *American Behavioral Scientist, 27*(1), 109–128.

Edelstein, L. (1943). *The Hippocratic Oath: Text, translation, and interpretation from the Greek*. Baltimore, MD: Johns Hopkins Press.

Gidman, W., Ward, P., & McGregor, L. (2012). Understanding public trust in services provided by community pharmacists relative to those provided by general practitioners: A qualitative study. *BMJ Open, 2*(3), 1–11.

Grant, D., & Alfred, K. C. (2007). Sanctions and recidivism: An evaluation of physician discipline by state medical boards. *Journal of Health Politics, Policy and Law, 32*(5), 867–885.

Harvey, G. (1686). *The conclave of physicians, detecting their intrigues, frauds and plots, against their patients* (2nd ed.). London: James Partridge.

Hulkower, R. (2016). The history of the Hippocratic Oath: Outdated, inauthentic, and yet still relevant. *Einstein Journal of Biology and Medicine, 25*(1), 41–44.

Iglehart, J. K. (2009). Finding money for health care reform: Rooting out waste, fraud, and abuse. *New England Journal of Medicine, 361*(3), 229–231.

Inman, T. (1861). *Foundation for a new theory & practice of medicine*. London: John Churchill.

Langbein, J. (1974). *Prosecuting crime in the Renaissance: England, Germany, France*. Cambridge: Harvard University Press.

Miles, S. H. (2005). *The Hippocratic Oath and the ethics of medicine*. Oxford: Oxford University Press.

Morris, L. (2009). Combating fraud in health care: An essential component of any cost containment strategy. *Health Affairs, 28*(5), 1351–1356.

Pande, V., & Maas, W. (2013). Physician Medicare fraud: Characteristics and consequences. *International Journal of Pharmaceutical and Healthcare Marketing, 7*(1), 8–33.

Payne, B. K. (2012). *White-collar crime: The essentials*. Thousand Oaks, CA: Sage Publications.

Policastro, C., & Payne, B. K. (2013). An examination of deviance and deviants in the durable *medical equipment* (DME) field: Characteristics, consequences, and responses to fraud. *Deviant Behavior, 34*(3), 191–207.

Robin, G. D. (1974). White-collar crime and employee theft. *Crime & Delinquency, 20*(3), 251–262.

Siegel, L. J. (2014). *Criminology: Theories, patterns, and typologies*. Toronto: Nelson Education.

Strader, J. K. (2011). *Understanding white collar crime*. Newark, NJ: LexisNexis.

Sutherland, E. H. (1949). *White collar crime*. New York: Dryden Press.

Sykes, G. M., & Matza, D. (1957). Techniques of neutralization: A theory of delinquency. *American Sociological Review, 22*(6), 664–670.

Tittle, C. R. (1995). *Control balance: Toward a general theory of deviance*. Boulder, CO: Westview Press.

Tittle, C. R. (2004). Refining control balance theory. *Theoretical Criminology, 8*(4), 395–428.

Wilson, P. R., Lincoln, R., & Chappell, D. (1986). Physician fraud and abuse in Canada: A preliminary examination. *Canadian Journal of Criminology, 28*(2), 129–146.

Wynia, M. K. (2008). The short history and tenuous future of medical professionalism: The erosion of medicine's social contract. *Perspectives in Biology and Medicine, 51*(4), 565–578.

2 Medical Insurance Fraud by Doctors

Beyond the prescription of unnecessary medical treatments (a point we return to in *Chapter 3*), theft and fraud, including underhanded billing and *medical equipment* schemes, represent the most pervasive and fastest growing white-collar crime trends in America's $2.5 trillion health care system (Centers for Medicare and Medicaid Services, 2015). The sheer size of this industry, especially the medical insurance sector, makes it a lucrative target for fraud and abuse (Sparrow, 2008). Estimates indicate that around a tenth of U.S. medical expenditures is wasted on fraud annually, amounting to upwards of $65 billion in losses per year (U.S. Government Accountability Office, 2018; National Health Care Anti-Fraud Association, 2012). This chapter presents an overview of the breadth and nature of fraudulent behaviors committed by physicians and applies contemporary criminological perspectives (i.e., routine activities theory and neutralization theory) to explain why physicians may engage in fraud.

Historically, no entity has suffered more losses to fraudster physicians than Medicare and Medicaid. Established under the 1965 Social Security Act, these federally subsidized health insurance programs were created to assist seniors, as well as lower-income and disabled persons (Berkowitz, 2005). Just eight years after their inception, the first exposé on overbilling and overtreatment scams among New York City physicians placed a spotlight on "bad doctors" (Jesilow, Pontell, & Geis, 1993). Disguised as a Medicaid recipient seeking treatment, *New York Daily News* reporter William Sherman uncovered evidence of doctors defrauding the public health system. In his twelve-part Pulitzer Prize-winning series, Sherman highlighted a wide range of unlawful and unethical clinician practices including (Sherman, 1973):

• "Cases in which doctors insisted that the patient fill prescriptions at a specific pharmacy even though Medicaid regulations demand that all patients be given a completely free choice of pharmacies."

(para. 4)

- "Psychiatrists who billed the city for more hours than there are in a day—one for as much as 35 hours of consultations in a single day."

(para. 4)

- "Ping-ponging of patients from doctor to doctor in several private owned group medical centers where the poor are rammed through an often needless but costly labyrinth of X-ray exams, lab tests, and dental care."

(para. 4)

Nearly 50 years have passed since then, yet Medicare and Medicaid fraud persists. In fact, it has become more expansive and complex (Bourgeon & Picard, 2014). Illustrating this rapid growth and prominence, in the summer of 2018, U.S. Attorney Jeff Sessions announced the largest health care fraud takedown in our nation's history. The Medicare Fraud Strike Force—an interagency task force consisting of investigators and prosecutors targeting the most egregious offenders engaged in health care fraud—along with the Federal Bureau of Investigation (FBI) and the Department of Justice (DOJ), enlisted the assistance of over 1,000 law enforcement officials across 58 federal districts to execute this historic takedown. Over 600 health care practitioners, including 165 physicians, were apprehended for their role in Medicare fraud and insurance billing schemes totaling more than $2 billion. These "trusted criminals" were charged with fraudulently billing for unnecessary treatment and procedures, many of which were never administered (DOJ, 2018).

Some of these rackets were solo ventures, whereas others involved highly sophisticated collusive networks. Examples of the corruptive physician acts include:

- Nearly 50 people in Texas were charged for their involvement in a $291 million fraud scheme. Among these defendants was a pharmacist charged with a drug and money laundering racket. According to the indictment, the pharmacist and his coconspirators (a pharmacy chain owner and managing partner) used fake prescriptions to fill bulk orders for over one million hydrocodone and oxycodone pills, which the pharmacy, in turn, sold to drug couriers for profit.

(DOJ, 2018)

- 35 defendants in Michigan were arrested for their roles in fraud, kickback, money laundering, and drug diversion schemes involving just under $200 million in false claims for medically unnecessary procedures or services never rendered. In one case, a doctor allegedly partnered with two home health agency owners in separate kickback scams, that resulted in over $12 million in fraudulent insurance claims.

(DOJ, 2018)

• 12 defendants across the state of Georgia, including two physicians, were charged for their involvement in several health care fraud, drug diversion, or compounding pharmacy schemes totaling more than $13.5 million in fraudulent billings.

(DOJ, 2018)

Similar to other white-collar crimes, medical insurance fraud is not a victimless offense. Likewise, this brand of deviance comes with far-reaching, deleterious consequences for insurance providers (e.g., economic toll) and patients (e.g., reduced insurance coverage). For one, it undermines the financial integrity and sustainability of public health programs, restricting the federal government's ability to provide affordable medical services to those most in need. Not to mention, more broadly, corrupt physician actions can also color public perceptions of medicine's legitimacy (Arnulf & Gottschalk, 2013; Perri, 2011).

Equally troubling, questionable medical practices jeopardize patient safety and access to quality health care services via reductions in medical coverage and higher copays and premiums (for individuals and employers). Further, eligibility changes for medical benefits flowing from false medical histories can cost patients dearly (Price & Norris, 2009). For example, false medical histories are often the result of physicians billing for services that were never rendered, leaving patients open to several problems. Disability benefits or life insurance policies may be wrongly denied, for instance. An inaccurate medical history might also affect treatment decisions and prompt some insurers to deny coverage benefits based on a "medical condition" found in the patient's record.

At this point, readers might ask: Why would doctors engage in such risky behavior? The incentive to generate income may be motivated by the fee-for-service (FFS) model in which physicians are reimbursed or paid for each service delivered to patients (Ash & Ellis, 2012; Byrd, Powell, & Smith, 2013), providing monetary incentive to maladaptive clinicians (see, e.g., Chaix-Couturier, Durand-Zaleski, Jolly, & Durieux, 2000). Put another way, that's where the money is! Given that the majority of third-party payers subscribe to this model, this offense carries both financial and health costs. For example, nearly 80% of employer-sponsored insurance plans in the U.S. utilize the FFS model (U.S. Bureau of Labor Statistics, 2010). Consequently, this payment arrangement contributes to a high volume of corruptive practices within the health care industry (Berwick & Hackbarth, 2012). In the section to come, we discuss the most common types of medical insurance crimes: fraudulent billing schemes and *medical equipment* fraud.

Billing Schemes

False claim schemes or billing schemes are the most common type of health insurance fraud (Appari & Johnson, 2010). *Medical billing fraud* occurs when physicians deliberately defraud insurers, in particular, Medicare, by filing fake invoices or billing statements for services never delivered to patients (Morris, 2009). Fraudulent billing is carried out through multiple avenues; however, the Centers for Medicare and Medicaid Services (CMS) (2015) indicate that the most frequent forms include: (1) upcoding, (2) unbundling, (3) phantom billing, and (4) double billing.

Upcoding, the most reported form of billing fraud, refers to an illegal practice in which medical providers or physicians bill for a more complex (and expensive) procedure than was actually administered (Payne, 2012). But how do they get away with this? When upcoding, maladaptive clinicians exploit victims through *current procedural terminology* (CPT) code manipulation. This code determines the dollar amount physicians will receive for each medical procedure performed. Rather than coding honestly, these upper-class offenders falsely bill insurance companies for more costly services.

Unbundling occurs when a physician separately bills for services, tests, or procedures that are usually bundled or packaged to collect more money from an insurance provider. When services are singly charged, the cost can be exponentially higher (Mashaw & Marmor, 1994). Imagine that you ordered a value meal at your local fast-food establishment. Instead of charging you the usual $3.99, the cashier charges you separately for each item, resulting in a price higher than normal. Although this is a trivialized depiction, it illustrates the way this form of fraud works. By separating the bundled services and coding for each, physicians seek to maximize the reimbursements from third-party insurers (Byrd et al., 2013).

Advances in electronic health records (EHR) software, though intended to increase the efficiency of record keeping and filesharing, have also made it easier for physicians to commit this type of fraud (Rosenbaum, Lopez, & Stifler, 2009). Computerized versions of patients' paper charts allow physicians real-time access to patient-specific records. While this access is beneficial to both health care providers and patients, deviant physicians can copy notes from a patient's previous appointments and paste these into each current treatment note. As a result, it appears as if the physician has diagnosed and treated every condition that is listed. Sometimes, offenders program their EHR software menus to reflect only treatment codes with the highest reimbursement rates (Rosenbaum et al., 2009).

Phantom billing takes place when physicians falsely bill insurers for procedures, services, or equipment that were either unnecessary or never delivered to clients (Payne, 2012). Medical examinations and tests performed usually depend on the conditions experienced by the patient. Those who engage in these practices deviate from this standard. A typical phantom billing scheme again involves physicians using EHR systems to automatically generate detailed patient observation profiles by copying and pasting notes from the records of other patients (Bowman, 2013). A recent example of this involves a New Jersey doctor, who according to U.S. Attorney Paul J. Fishman, was the ringleader in a three-year phantom billing scheme (DOJ, 2015). The defendant stole roughly $240,000 from Medicare and Medicaid by filing phantom claims for physical therapy services never rendered. In many instances, deviant physicians also commit other crimes that are often related to fraud. This was the case with this defendant, as he was also charged with tax evasion.

Double billing is another significant issue encountered by Medicare, private insurers, and patients. Physicians who duplicate charges for the same service or procedure are double-billing insurance providers (Payne, 2012). Oftentimes, multiple insurers, including Medicare and private insurance companies, as well as the patient are billed for duplicate services. In some cases, physicians charge more than once for the same service. For example, a doctor in Virginia pled guilty to double-billing insurers. This clinician authorized *superbills*—a form that determines the services to charge a health care insurer for. He doubled-billed providers for "evaluation and management" and "preventative counseling" services for the same patient visit (DOJ, 2017). Other instances involve multiple physicians seeking reimbursement for services rendered to the same patient for the same procedure on the same day.

Medical Equipment Fraud

Partnerships between physicians and the health care industry (e.g., biotech and equipment manufacturers and distributors) can enrich the medical field and benefit patients. Physicians contribute to the development, testing, and training vital to producing safe and effective *medical equipment* via feedback, research, and clinical trials, and participating in medical education programs. In most instances, physicians are compensated by equipment manufacturers legitimately for their intellectual contributions toward the development of innovative medical products. The opportunities to quickly accumulate money through lucrative royalty contracts, consulting agreements, stock options, and research funding have challenged the integrity of some physicians, causing some to put personal profit over principles. Experts warn that these business arrangements can contaminate medical decision-making (Coyle, 2002; Korn & Carlat, 2013). Gelberman, Samson, Mirza, Callaghan, and Pellegrini (2010) contend that such partnerships shape physician behavior by fostering a setting in which there is motivation to reciprocate for even small gifts (e.g., free lunches, subsidized trips, and drug samples). Even those who lack deceptive intentions are often unconsciously swayed by highly attractive perquisites (Korn & Carlat, 2013). Whether in a hospital, clinic, or private practice setting, physicians usually decide or heavily influence decisions about the equipment used for procedures. For these reasons, *medical equipment* manufacturers utilize sales and marketing schemes meant to entice physicians into selecting or recommending their product. A remarkably large share of these companies readily resort to unlawful tactics, normally in the form of kickbacks, to prompt compliance.

Physicians who accept kickbacks or other under-the-table incentives from *medical equipment* companies in exchange for product referrals—often without concern for quality or safety—are engaging in a type of *medical equipment fraud*. Such payments might present dilemmas for some physicians in which their own self-interests are placed at odds with the interests of patients. Medical decision-making commingled with egocentrism, privilege, and prerogative is a potentially dangerous brew for patients (Pellegrino & Relman, 1999). We have seen such disregard for the profession and patient safety in cases where physicians refer faulty or unnecessary products based solely on profitable opportunities offered by *medical equipment* businesses (Campbell, 2007; Moses & Jones, 2018).

Before we delve deeper into this topic, we should first clarify what counts as *medical equipment*. *Medical equipment* (ME) can range from stents to wheelchairs to surgical implants (see Table 2.1). The U.S. Food and Drug Administration (FDA) classifies ME as durable and non-durable and

Table 2.1 Medical Equipment Classifications

Equipment Classification	Examples
Class I (low risk)	Elastic bandages, examination gloves, hand-held surgical instruments
Class II (moderate risk)	Powered wheelchairs, infusion pumps, surgical drapes
Class III (high risk)	Heart valves, silicone gel-filled breast implants, implanted cerebella stimulators

Source: U.S. FDA (2018)

defines it as any self- or clinician-operated instrument, apparatus, machine, or other accessory intended for the diagnosis, cure, treatment, or prevention of diseases or conditions (U.S. FDA, 2018). *Medical equipment* is considered durable if it can withstand repeated use (e.g., hospital beds, respirators, bedside commodes, and apnea monitors), whereas non-durable equipment such as diabetic test strips, syringes, diapers, and catheters are disposable and cannot withstand repeated use (CMS, 2015).

Of the products utilized in the health care industry, durable *medical equipment* (DME) is not only the costliest, but clearly represents the area that is most open to medical fraud (Policastro & Payne, 2013). According to the U.S. Government Accountability Office (GAO) (2018), in comparison to other types of service providers, DME providers are responsible for a large amount of improper payments. The estimated annual financial loss from DME fraud is quite high, dramatically increasing from $1.5 billion to $5 billion per year since 2009 (National Insurance Crime Bureau, 2012).

The U.S. *medical equipment* market is the largest globally, as reports from Datamonitor reveal the revenue generated totaled more than $110 billion in 2015 alone (see Figure 2.1).[1] Given the money-making opportunities and proximity, it seems somewhat inevitable that physicians and *medical equipment* companies have formed profitable alliances. Over the last decade, the *medical equipment* industry has experienced a steady rise in sales (CMS, 2017). The allure of this lucrative market is not difficult to comprehend and may largely explain the proliferation of physician-owned

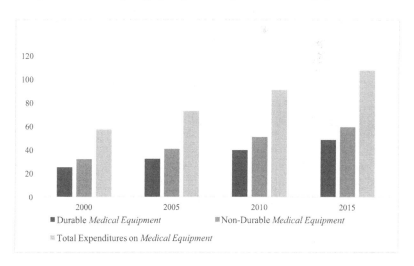

Figure 2.1 U.S. *Medical Equipment* Expenditures, 2000–2015 (Billions of dollars)

Source: NHE data from the Centers for Medicare and Medicaid Services (2017)

distributorships (PODs) and investments in this sector in recent years (Leder-haus, 2011). Though POD proponents tout the benefits, many authorities have voiced concerns over this trend, suggesting that such business ventures cultivate an anti-competitive market and raise quality of care concerns. In addition to POD-related schemes, various other forms of *medical equipment* fraud exist such as billing for unnecessary equipment or phantom supplies. Other deceptive acts involve doctors invoicing for more expensive equipment than was actually delivered to patients. Physicians involved in this type of fraud also accept kickbacks from suppliers on referrals and submit falsified claims for nonexistent patients (e.g., using deceased persons' social security numbers). To provide a glimpse into the layers of complexity and deception in DME fraud, we highlight the following case:

> In June 2014, a San Francisco physician was sentenced to two years in prison and ordered to pay over $1.5 million in restitution for accepting kickbacks. Court documents reveal that over the span of five years, recruiters from a power wheel chair provider submitted over 400 false power wheelchair claims to Medicare. The names of beneficiaries were derived from bogus prescriptions and medical records prepared by the doctor. In return for his role, the physician was paid a $100 kickback for each power wheelchair prescription.
>
> (U.S. Department of Health and Human Services, 2014)

Theoretical Explanations of Physician Fraud

While the emergence of the white-collar crime concept can be traced back as far as the late 1890s (Ross, 1907), literature concerning this kind of crime within the health care system remains sparse. Despite the similarities of physician fraud to other white-collar offenses, the applicability of crime theories within this realm is relatively underexplored (Perri, Lichtenwald, & Mieczkowska, 2014). As a subfield of white-collar crime, the study of physician deviance naturally calls for criminological insights. In this section, we offer theoretical perspectives that might explain such behavior. Although an exhaustive overview is outside the purview of this text, we briefly cover two of the more suitable rationales from the economic crime research tradition: 1) routine activities theory and 2) neutralization theory.

Routine Activities Theory

A logical framework for understanding the role of doctors in health care fraud is Cohen and Felson's (1979) routine activities theory (RAT). Originally developed to explain predatory offending, RAT is also applicable to

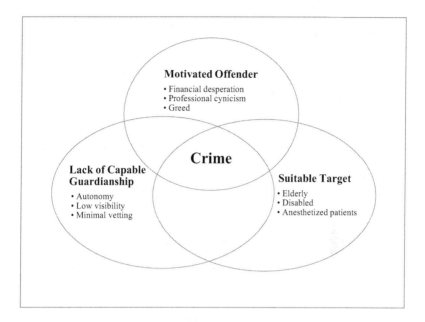

Figure 2.2 Routine Activities Theory Matrix

white-collar offending, including physician misconduct. In the simplest terms, RAT proposes that crime stems from the convergence of motivated offenders and suitable targets in settings where capable guardianship is missing (see Figure 2.2). With respect to Medicare and Medicaid fraud, the health insurance sector's operational structure puts deviant physicians in close proximity to their prospective targets in unsupervised spaces. That is, offending physicians, owing mostly to a healthy profit motive, exploit the sophisticated and ambiguous claims process at the expense of providers and patients.

Testifying to the financial lure of physician fraud, the extant literature shows that like other white-collar offenders (see Thio, 2001), deviant doctors often run afoul of the law because of financial hardships and greed (Hoffmann, 2009). Adding to this, former DOJ prosecutor, Gejaa Gobena, provided much needed insights into the motivation behind these crimes during a recent Medscape Medical News interview (Lowes, 2016, n.p.):

> I think that the most common factor is financial difficulty. Sometimes it intersects with another factor, which is age. Because you have a doctor in a tough financial situation towards the end of their career,

participating in these schemes gives them a way to make some money very quickly . . . Oftentimes it is personal bankruptcy, or someone who's been married a couple times, got divorced, has various alimony or child support obligations.

Scholars have also found that inadequate guardianship or operational oversight makes the insurance sector ripe for white-collar deviance (Jesilow, Geis, & Pontell, 1991). For instance, in one of the most influential articles on physician crime, *Fraud by Physicians Against Medicaid*, Jesilow and colleagues' (1991) interviews of over 40 fraudster doctors revealed that the income-generating potential and relative ease of getting away with violations made these exploitative opportunities highly tempting. Highlighting a lack of capable guardianship, they also disclosed that no one verified the claims they filed, leading them to operate without much concern about being caught.

Nearly 30 years later under the current FFS system, the veracity of claims is still generally assumed (in the absence of obvious discrepancies), resulting in reimbursements being paid with minimal vetting (McGee, Sandridge, Treadway, Vance, & Coustasse, 2018). Further, computerized claims processing systems allow bad doctors to offend without ever having personal contact with insurance providers. Considering these conditions, in tandem with the low risk of detection, doctors find themselves in environments highly conducive to impropriety and fraud.

The average patient's lack of extensive medical training and knowledge, along with an interminable trust in physicians (Hoffmann, 2009), provide these motivated offenders with a ready supply of suitable targets. Vulnerable patients in particular (e.g., the poor, less-educated, and the elderly) retain greater risks of being victimized at the hands of doctors (DuBois et al., 2012; Kastenbaum, 2015). Without sufficient guardianship, the enigmatical nature of medical profession norms (DuBois et al., 2012), conjoined with the complexities and confusion surrounding health care networks and insurance billing (Jesilow et al., 1993), allow deviant physicians to operate easily under concealment from others (Benson, Madensen, & Eck, 2009).

Importantly, the presence of all three elements does not signify the inevitability of crime. RAT instead identifies the relationship between crime and the coexistence of these three elements (Cohen & Felson, 1979). Unlike other offender-centered crime theories, RAT contends that reducing criminal opportunities mitigates crime (Miller, 2012). In other words, a deficiency in one of these conditions reduces the odds of victimization, an insight that might serve medical fraud prevention initiatives well. We will revisit this idea in *Chapter 5* when discussing potential strategies that may reduce the prevalence of fraud in the medical field.

Neutralization Theory

Another criminological theory that may prove useful in understanding deviant medical decision-making is Sykes and Matza's (1957) techniques of neutralization perspective. Neutralization theory was developed to explain how juveniles, who otherwise subscribe to conventional value systems, vacillate between conformity and delinquency (Matza, 1964). In contrast to Cohen's (1955) subcultural theory of delinquency, Sykes and Matza (1957) challenged the prevailing notion that deviants and law-abiding citizens subscribe to a different set of values, maintaining that their norms are more homogeneous than not. According to this perspective, crime occurs when otherwise prosocial persons (e.g., doctors) are able to suppress or neutralize conventional values and engage in malfeasance.

As Sykes and Matza (1957) theorize, people employ neutralization techniques that allow them to overcome moral hurdles that would normally prevent them from engaging in criminal activities (Kieffer & Sloan, 2009). By minimizing guilt, neutralizations eliminate the stigma associated with criminality and, thus, allow for the maintenance of a positive self-image, irrespective of one's criminal culpability (Matza, 1964). Among people with conventional values, Agnew and Peters (1986) argue that deviance occurs when people accept a technique of neutralization and believe they are in a situation where the neutralization applies.

Sykes and Matza (1957) spelled out five neutralizing techniques used by offenders: 1) denial of responsibility, 2) denial of injury, 3) denial of victim, 4) condemning the condemners, and 5) appeal to higher loyalties (Sykes & Matza, 1957). The first three techniques are rather straightforward. Denial of responsibility refers to individuals defining themselves as lacking culpability for their maladaptive behaviors. This technique is exemplified by the idea that the crime was not the offender's fault, rather an accident or the fault of forces beyond his/her control (e.g., poor upbringing). Sykes and Matza (1957) equate this to a "billiard ball" conception of self where the offender views him/herself as being more acted upon than acting (p. 667). Denial of injury occurs when individuals, despite the fact their behavior is contrary to law, feel their actions did not negatively impact others or may redefine their behaviors as something other than criminal. For instance, the offender may draw attention to the fact that no one was physically hurt by their fraudulent behavior or they were "borrowing" money rather than stealing it. The next technique, denial of victim, concerns the transference of blame to victims. In many cases, victims belonging to certain ostracized subgroups (e.g., prostitutes, drug addicts, minorities, and the poor) are not viewed as victims by mainstream society, and as a microcosm of the greater society, doctors are not immune to such biases (see e.g., Chapman, Kaatz, & Carnes, 2013).

Condemning the condemners describes justifications of wrongdoing in which misconduct is considered retaliatory and ensuing benefits are believed to be deserved. This technique ultimately shifts the focus of blame from the offender to those in power who have created the rules and regulations that govern society, and in this context, the medical field. Because corruption exists in America's systems (Kieffer & Sloan, 2009), offenders, particularly those with white-collars, oftentimes justify their actions by assigning blame to policy and lawmakers, as well as the government for their misdeeds (Benson, 1985). Offenders often argue that they are not the problem, rather the broken and corrupt system is the issue. In the medical sphere, common complaints among physicians include low reimbursement rates and bureaucratic constraints on patient care decisions (Jesilow et al., 1993). Perhaps a respondent in Jesilow and colleagues' (1993) study of criminal doctors puts it best:

> They've built in systems that either ask for somebody to cheat . . . or to cheat the patient on the type of care that's provided. You put somebody in the position where lying is the most reasonable course, and they will lie. The patients will lie; the doctor may even lie on what they say about what happened.
>
> (p. 155)

Other scholars note that "a subculture of medical delinquency . . . arises, thrives, and grows in large part because of the tension between bureaucratic regulation and professional norms of autonomy" (Pogrebin, 2007, p. 156). Notably, these reigning attitudes have not only been observed among physicians but have been found in medical student groups as well. Case in point, in a study conducted by Keenan, Brown, Pontell, and Geis (1985), students insisted that constraints stemming from the governing regulations and policies of Medicare promoted fraudulent behavior among physicians.

Lastly, the technique of appealing to higher loyalties is commonly utilized by deviant physicians (DuBois et al., 2012; Hoffmann, 2009). Centered on the hierarchy of loyalty, offenders sacrifice the demands of greater society for the demands of their own subgroup and clients (Sykes & Matza, 1957). Examples of this type of rationalization in health care was observed in Wynia, Cummins, VanGeest, and Wilson's (2000) study of 720 practicing physicians. Because of health care coverage limitations, some respondents "gamed" the reimbursement system as a form of patient advocacy. For instance, while some physicians falsely billed providers for a covered procedure or treatment, other clinicians embellished or misrepresented the severity of patients' conditions to help them secure coverage (Wynia et al., 2000). Though neutralizations may not fully shield the individual from the force of his own internalized values and the reactions of conforming others

(Sykes & Matza, 1957), such rationalizations provide episodic relief from moral quandaries that constrain deviant behavior. Since white-collar physicians otherwise tend to be law-abiding, highly trusted pillars of the community (Presser, 2009), neutralization theory provides a viable framework for examining physician deviance.

Conclusion

Fraudulent behavior by physicians encompasses a diverse range of schemes that exact an immense financial cost to patients and society as a whole. According to the GAO (2018), Medicare paid out an estimated $52 billion in improper payments during fiscal year 2017. Importantly, given that this figure includes a broad array of situations that may not involve fraud such as payments made in the incorrect amount or made in complete error (U.S. GAO, 2018), improper payments are only a proxy of the extent of fraud. However, this staggering figure indicates the potential impact of a single program, albeit one of the largest payers of health care benefits in the United States (CMS, 2017). Demonstrating its immense size, Medicare provided coverage for over 58 million people in 2017 (U.S. GAO, 2018). Current projections indicate that Medicare's hospital insurance trust fund will be depleted by 2026 which will undoubtedly affect the lives of millions of patients who depend upon it for health care (CMS, 2018). Fraud, including the offenses committed by physicians, is an issue that contributes to wasteful spending in our country's health care system and more attention is needed in order to reduce fraudulent claims and practices. Criminological theory, as presented in previous sections, may hold important insights into reducing and preventing fraud by physicians in our current health care system.

Note

1. Datamonitor is an international corporation that provides market intelligence and data analysis of pharmaceutical and biotechnology industries (Eliades, Retterath, Hueltenschmidt, & Singh, 2012).

References

Agnew, R., & Peters, A. A. (1986). The techniques of neutralization: An analysis of predisposing and situational factors. *Criminal Justice and Behavior, 13*(1), 81–97.

Appari, A., & Johnson, M. E. (2010). Information security and privacy in healthcare: Current state of research. *International Journal of Internet and Enterprise Management, 6*(4), 279–314.

Arnulf, J. K., & Gottschalk, P. (2013). Heroic leaders as white-collar criminals: An empirical study. *Journal of Investigative Psychology and Offender Profiling*, *1*(10), 96–113.

Ash, A. S., & Ellis, R. P. (2012). Risk-adjusted payment and performance assessment for primary care. *Medical Care*, *50*(8), 643–653.

Benson, M. L. (1985). Denying the guilty mind: Accounting for involvement in a white-collar crime. *Criminology*, *23*(4), 583–607.

Benson, M. L., Madensen, T. D., & Eck, J. E. (2009). *White-collar crime from an opportunity perspective*. New York: Springer.

Berkowitz, E. (2005). Medicare and Medicaid: The past as prologue. *Health Care Financing Review*, *27*(2), 11–24.

Berwick, D. M., & Hackbarth, A. D. (2012). Eliminating waste in US health care. *JAMA*, *307*(14), 1513–1516.

Bourgeon, J. M., & Picard, P. (2014). Fraudulent claims and nitpicky insurers. *American Economic Review*, *104*(9), 2900–2917.

Bowman, S. (2013). Impact of electronic health record systems on information integrity: Quality and safety implications. *Perspectives in Health Information Management*, *10*(1c), 1–19.

Byrd, J. D., Powell, P., & Smith, D. L. (2013). Health care fraud: An introduction to a major cost issue. *Journal of Accounting, Ethics, & Public Policy*, *14*, 522–539.

Campbell, E. G. (2007). Doctors and drug companies: Scrutinizing influential relationships. *New England Journal of Medicine*, *357*(18), 1796–1797.

Centers for Medicare and Medicaid Services. (2015). *Preventing fraud, waste, and abuse in home health services and durable medical equipment*. Retrieved from www.cms.gov/medicare-medicaid-coordination/fraud-prevention/medicaid-integrity-education/provider-education-toolkits/downloads/prevent-fraud-durablemedicalequip.pdf

Centers for Medicare and Medicaid Services. (2017). *National health expenditure data*. Retrieved from www.cms.gov/research-statistics-data-and-systems/statistics-trends-and-reports/nationalhealthexpenddata/nationalhealthaccountshistorical.html

Centers for Medicare and Medicaid Services. (2018). *The 2018 boards of trustees, federal hospital insurance and federal supplementary medical insurance trust funds*. Retrieved from www.cms.gov/Research-Statistics-Data-and-Systems/Statistics-Trends-and-Reports/ReportsTrustFunds/Downloads/TR2018.pdf

Chaix-Couturier, C., Durand-Zaleski, I., Jolly, D., & Durieux, P. (2000). Effects of financial incentives on medical practice: Results from a systematic review of the literature and methodological issues. *International Journal for Quality in Health Care*, *12*(2), 133–142.

Chapman, E. N., Kaatz, A., & Carnes, M. (2013). Physicians and implicit bias: How doctors may unwittingly perpetuate health care disparities. *Journal of General Internal Medicine*, *28*(11), 1504–1510.

Cohen, L. E. (1955). *Delinquent boys: The culture of the gang*. New York: Simon & Schuster.

Cohen, L. E., & Felson, M. (1979). Social change and crime rate trends: A routine activity approach. *American Sociological Review*, *44*(4), 588–608.

Coyle, S. L. (2002). Physician: Industry relations: Individual physicians. *Annals of Internal Medicine, 136*(5), 396–402.

Department of Justice. (2015). *Doctor sentenced to 16 months in prison for taking bribes in test-referral scheme with New Jersey clinical lab.* Retrieved from www. justice.gov/usao-nj/pr/doctor-sentenced-16-months-prison-taking-bribes-test-referral-scheme-new-jersey-clinical

Department of Justice. (2017). *Danville doctor pleads guilty to healthcare fraud, tax evasion charges.* Retrieved from www.justice.gov/usao-wdva/pr/danville-doctor-pleads-guilty-healthcare-fraud-tax-evasion-charges

Department of Justice. (2018). *National health care fraud takedown results in charges against 601 individuals responsible for over $2 billion in fraud losses.* Retrieved from www.justice.gov/opa/pr/national-health-care-fraud-takedown-results-charges-against-601-individuals-responsible-over

DuBois, J. M., Anderson, E. E., Carroll, K., Gibb, T., Kraus, E., Rubbelke, T., & Vasher, M. (2012). Environmental factors contributing to wrongdoing in medicine: A criterion-based review of studies and cases. *Ethics & Behavior, 22*(3), 163–188.

Eliades, G., Retterath, M., Hueltenschmidt, N., & Singh, K. (2012). *Healthcare 2020.* Retrieved from https://www.bain.com/contentassets/063d85be0237467fab e711835fb36e7d/bain_brief_healthcare_2020.pdf

Gelberman, R. H., Samson, D., Mirza, S. K., Callaghan, J. J., & Pellegrini, V. D. (2010). Orthopaedic surgeons and the medical device industry. *The Journal of Bone and Joint Surgery, 92*(3), 765–777.

Hoffmann, D. E. (2009). Physicians who break the law. *St. Louis University Law Journal, 53*(4), 1049–1088.

Jesilow, P., Geis, G., & Pontell, H. (1991). Fraud by physicians against Medicaid. *JAMA, 266*(23), 3318–3322.

Jesilow, P., Pontell, H. N., & Geis, G. (1993). *Prescription for profit: How doctors defraud Medicaid.* Berkeley: University of California Press.

Kastenbaum, R. J. (2015). *Death, society, and human experience.* London: Routledge.

Keenan, C. E., Brown, G. C., Pontell, H. N., & Geis, G. (1985). Medical students' attitudes on physician fraud and abuse in the Medicare and Medicaid programs. *Academic Medicine, 60*(3), 167–173.

Kieffer, S. M., & Sloan, J. J. (2009). Overcoming moral hurdles: Using techniques of neutralization by white-collar suspects as an interrogation tool. *Security Journal, 22*(4), 317–330.

Korn, D., & Carlat, D. (2013). Conflicts of interest in medical education: Recommendations from the pew task force on medical conflicts of interest. *JAMA, 310*(22), 2397–2398.

Lederhaus, S. C. (2011). Physician-owned distributors: The wave of the future or the end of the model? *Ethics in Biology, Engineering and Medicine: An International Journal, 2*(3), 279–293.

Lowes, R. (2016, October 12). Former prosecutor profiles the criminal physician. *Medscape News.* Retrieved from www.medscape.com/viewarticle/870155

22 *Medical Insurance Fraud by Doctors*

Mashaw, J. L., & Marmor, T. R. (1994). Conceptualizing, estimating, and reform-
ing fraud, waste, and abuse in healthcare spending. *Yale Journal on Regulation,*
11(2), 455–494.
Matza, D. (1964). *Drift.* New York: John Wiley & Sons.
McGee, J., Sandridge, L., Treadway, C., Vance, K., & Coustasse, A. (2018). Strate-
gies for fighting Medicare fraud. *The Health Care Manager, 37*(2), 147–154.
Miller, J. (2012). Individual offending, routine activities, and activity settings:
Revisiting the routine activity theory of general deviance. *Journal of Research in*
Crime and Delinquency, 50(3), 390–416.
Morris, L. (2009). Combating fraud in health care: An essential component of any
cost containment strategy. *Health Affairs, 28*(5), 1351–1356.
Moses, R. E., & Jones, D. S. (2018). Health care fraud and the essentials to avoid
problems. *The American Journal of Gastroenterology, 113,* 1277–1279.
National Health Care Anti-Fraud Association. (2012). *The problem of health care*
fraud. Washington, DC: NHCAA.
National Insurance Crime Bureau. (2012). *ForeCast report: Report on durable*
medical equipment. Retrieved from www.nicb.org/File%20Library/Public%20
Affairs/DME-ForeCAST_PUBLIC_1-24-12.pdf
Payne, B. K. (2012). *White-collar crime: The essentials.* Thousand Oaks, CA: Sage
Publications.
Pellegrino, E. D., & Relman, A. S. (1999). Professional medical associations: Ethi-
cal and practical guidelines. *JAMA, 282*(10), 984–986.
Perri, F. S. (2011). White-collar criminals: The "kinder, gentler" offender? *Journal*
of Investigative Psychology and Offender Profiling, 8(3), 217–241.
Perri, F. S., Lichtenwald, T. G., & Mieczkowska, E. M. (2014). Sutherland, Cleckley
and beyond: White-collar crime and psychopathy. *International Journal of Psy-*
chological Studies, 6(4), 71–88.
Pogrebin, M. (2007). *A view of the offender's world about criminals.* New York:
Sage Publications.
Policastro, C., & Payne, B. K. (2013). An examination of deviance and deviants in
the durable *medical equipment* (DME) field: Characteristics, consequences, and
responses to fraud. *Deviant Behavior, 34*(3), 191–207.
Presser, L. (2009). The narratives of offenders. *Theoretical Criminology, 13*(2),
177–200.
Price, M., & Norris, D. M. (2009). Health care fraud: Physicians as white collar
criminals? *Journal of the American Academy of Psychiatry and the Law, 37*(3),
286–289.
Rosenbaum, S. J., Lopez, N., & Stifler, S. (2009). *Health care fraud.* Washington,
DC: George Washington University.
Ross, E. A. (1907). *Sin and society: An analysis of latter-day iniquity.* New York:
Harper and Row.
Sherman, W. (1973, January 28). The city's Medicaid system: Still sick, sick,
sick. *The New York Times.* Retrieved from http://sites.dlib.nyu.edu/undercover/
sites/dlib.nyu.edu.undercover/files/documents/uploads/editors/NYDailyNews_
1973Jan23_pg7.pdf

Sparrow, M. K. (2008). Fraud in the US health-care system: Exposing the vulnerabilities of automated payments systems. *Social Research: An International Quarterly, 75*(4), 1151–1180.

Sykes, G. M., & Matza, D. (1957). Techniques of neutralization: A theory of delinquency. *American Sociological Review, 22*(6), 664–670.

Thio, A. (2001). *Deviant behavior* (6th ed.). Boston: Allyn and Bacon.

U.S. Bureau of Labor Statistics. (2010). *Program perspectives: Features and associated costs of fee-for-service medical plans.* Retrieved from www.bls.gov/opub/btn/archive/program-perspectives-on-fee-for-service-plans.pdf

U.S. Department of Health and Human Services. (2014). *Health care fraud and abuse control program annual report.* Retrieved from http://oig.hhs.gov/publications/docs/hcfac/FY2014-hcfac.pdf

U.S. Food and Drug Administration. (2018). *Medical devices.* Retrieved from www.fda.gov/MedicalDevices/

U.S. Government Accountability Office. (2018). *Actions needed to mitigate billions in improper payments and program integrity risks.* Retrieved from www.gao.gov/assets/700/692821.pdf

Wynia, M. K., Cummins, D. S., VanGeest, J. B., & Wilson, I. B. (2000). Physician manipulation of reimbursement rules for patients: Between a rock and a hard place. *JAMA, 283*(14), 1858–1865.

3 Violence by Doctors Against Patients

It is safe to suggest that most patients are aware of the main maxim of the Hippocratic Oath, "First do no harm." Thus, headlines and exposés that draw attention to physicians who have abused their patients often result in shock and outrage. To shed additional light on an understudied phenomenon, this chapter focuses on two forms of physical violence doctors may commit against their patients: sexual abuse and unnecessary surgeries. We argue that unnecessary procedures[1] constitute a form of violence against patients as these "treatments" are invasive and can result in both short- and long-term physical injury. Other scholars have offered a similar argument (see Friedrichs, 2010; Jesilow et al., 1985). Recent high-profile cases have called attention to physicians who were clearly taking advantage of their patients and violating the trust our society often places in health care providers. Notably, the Larry Nassar case has demonstrated to the nation, and the world, that sexual victimization can occur at the hands of trusted medical professionals.

In 2018, a judge ordered Nassar to serve a sentence of 40 to 175 years in prison for criminal sexual conduct against ten victims, all of whom were under the age of 16, including three who were under 13 years old at the time of the offense. The vast majority of victims were sexually assaulted while attending an appointment with Nassar (Adams, 2018). In all, 156 women, including accomplished Olympic gymnasts, testified at his sentencing hearing, relaying stories of extensive sexual abuse at the doctor's hands over the span of his career (*The Guardian*, 2018). Fortunately, studies suggest that violence and abuse by doctors is a relatively rare phenomenon, especially when compared to other forms of misconduct (see Arora, Douglas, & Goold, 2014). A small fraction of physicians, however, does engage in this type of behavior, signifying the importance of considering not only the nature of this form of deviance, but potential explanations for such behaviors as well.

Unnecessary Procedures

Of the procedures performed by physicians, surgeries are considered by far the most lucrative and dangerous (Hogan, 2016). *Unnecessary surgeries* are defined as "any surgical intervention that is either not needed, not indicated, or not in the patient's best interest when weighed against other available options, including conservative measures" (Stahel, VanderHeiden, & Kim, 2017, p. 1). Unwarranted surgeries represent a problem of astounding proportions particularly related to needless pain, suffering, and death, as well as a substantial waste of human and financial resources (Leape, 1989). In an observational study based on a sample of over 2,000 clinicians, respondents reported that they felt anywhere from 30% to 45% of health care was "unnecessary," with roughly 16% believing that upwards to half of all medical procedures were not needed (Lyu et al., 2017). Other current estimates suggest that nearly 20 to 30% of all surgeries are unwarranted (Kelley, 2009). Demonstrating the willingness of some physicians to expose patients to risks of iatrogenic[2] illness, injury, or death, the most common forms of unnecessary surgeries include: the removal of tonsils and appendixes, cardiac surgeries, hysterectomies, and cesarean sections (Friedrichs, 2010). Narrowing the focus down to the more jeopardous of the noted procedures, we review several cases involving questionable surgeries below:

• In 2000, in a study concerning recommendations for hysterectomies in California, it was discovered that surgery was inappropriately prescribed in about 70% of cases.

(Bernstein, 2000)

• In a 2009 study of patients who received an implantable cardioverter-defibrillator (ICD), researchers reported that there was no evidence to support the surgical installation of these devices in almost a quarter of the cases.

(Al-Khatib et al., 2011)

• Cesarean deliveries represent the most commonly performed surgical procedure in the U.S., with much variability existing in the rates of C-sections occurring across the nation. Even when expectant mothers retain low risks of complications, this delivery method is overused.

(Kozhimannil, Law, & Virnig, 2013)

The costs of unnecessary medical procedures impact the government, insurance providers, and patients. In an era of mandatory reporting in the medical sphere, health care providers are required to report every procedurally related error; however, neither the federal nor state governments track unnecessary medical procedures or their consequences. This can include infections (e.g., sepsis) or other complications (e.g., damaged artery or overexposure to radiation) which in turn can lead to severe disability or even death (Singh et al., 2013).[3] Unnecessary medical procedures cost the U.S. health care system over $150 billion yearly and account for nearly a third of the nation's total health care expenditures (Smith, Saunders, Stuckhardt, & McGinnis, 2013).

While needless surgeries may be the most frightening and invasive of unnecessary medical procedures, there is also growing concern nationwide regarding the volume of tests, procedures, and operations performed by physicians (Mehta, Tribble, & Mehta, 2011). *Unnecessary medical procedures* are described as health care treatments, tests, or services provided without evidence that such practices will be of benefit to patients (Smith et al., 2013). That is, unnecessary medical procedures are those services not supported by research, duplicative, potentially harmful, or not essential (Levinson et al., 2015), and include, but are not limited to, lab tests, X-rays, CAT scans, angioplasties, and cesarean sections. In a 2015 study conducted by Levinson and colleagues, three-quarters of the sampled physicians indicated that unnecessary tests and procedures are a major issue, and more than seven out of ten disclosed that on average, physicians prescribe an unnecessary diagnostic test at least once a week. This problem plagues the medical industry and is further evidenced by the more than 1,000 physicians who have made payments to settle malpractice suits in cases involving claims of unsubstantiated procedures over the past 14 years. Nearly half of these cases included allegations of serious permanent injury or death, and in many instances, involved multiple plaintiffs (U. S. Department of Health and Human Services, 2014).

While these incidences and correlated risks are apparent, reform has been slow (Leape, 2015b). It is possible that the financial incentives may be too great, and thus, partly responsible for the pervasiveness of such practices. As the number of surgeries and other procedures increase, hospitals and physicians also experience an upsurge in revenue. Perhaps even more disturbing is the fact that when complications arise from these unwarranted treatments, from a financial perspective, health care facilities reap greatly (Leape, 2015a). As was previously discussed, most practitioners within the health care industry subscribe to the FFS model, and since physician incomes are largely dependent on the number of procedures performed, there is unremitting pressure to generate revenue (Oberlander & Laugesen, 2015).

Similar to other forms of physician deviance, the repercussions of unnecessary medical procedures often adversely affect Medicare and those covered under its policies. For instance, Welch, Hayes, and Frost (2012) evaluated the prevalence of 26 commonly overused procedures that have been found to have little to no medical benefit. This was the first large-scale investigation of Medicare expenditures associated with procedures widely regarded as inessential (e.g., advanced imaging for simple lower back pain to implanting stents in patients with stable heart disease). Findings indicate that over 40% of Medicare beneficiaries were subjected to at least one of these procedures, costing the government about $8.5 billion.[4] In another study, Eappen et al. (2013) demonstrated that complications stemming from unneeded surgeries performed on privately and publicly insured patients yield more earnings for physicians and hospitals than those with alternate coverage. There are a number of factors that contribute to this problem (e.g., insistent patient requests, malpractice concerns, and fear of misdiagnoses), yet the American health care system structure, along with its focus on profit, is likely to heavily influence the number of unnecessary procedures taking place in medical facilities across the nation (Mehta et al., 2011). As we close this section, notice the following cases illustrating the types of unnecessary procedures performed by physicians deemed criminal in nature:

- In the latter part of 2014, a New York cardiologist was ordered to serve three years in prison and pay $2 million in restitution after accepting a plea deal for health care fraud. According to the indictment, the cardiologist built his clientele by trading patients' narcotic prescriptions in exchange for them agreeing to undergo pointless testing and other medical procedures. In addition to filing invoices for fabricated office visits and patient diagnoses, he also falsely billed both private and public health insurers for these unneeded services.
  (U.S. Department of Health and Human Services, 2015)

- During the summer of 2015, a hematologist-oncologist based in the Detroit metropolitan area was sentenced to 45 years behind bars and forced to hand over roughly $18 million for his leading role in a health care fraud, money laundering, and kickback scheme involving over 550 victimized patients. Court records indicate that the defendant administered medically unnecessary treatments such as chemotherapy and intravenous iron therapy. Many of these patients suffered serious side effects following these unneeded treatments. Facilitated through his numerous diagnostic facilities and cancer clinics statewide, the defendant admitted to running money laundering and kickback rackets. In all, this criminal physician swindled Medicare, Blue Cross Blue Shield of Michigan, and other insurers out of approximately $34 million.
  (U.S. Department of Health and Human Services, 2015)

- In the spring of 2015, a multiple site cardiology practice located in New Jersey found itself out of nearly $4 million for alleged Civil False Claim Act violations. This medical group was targeted for the illegal company-wide practice of subjecting patients to and billing Medicare for unnecessary cardiology tests and procedures, including stress tests and cardiac catheterizations.

(U.S. Department of Health and Human Services, 2015)

Explaining Unnecessary Procedures by Doctors

A key question that arises when considering the pervasiveness of unnecessary surgeries and procedures is: Why would a doctor who is duty-bound to protect patients' interests engage in these risky, and in some cases potentially fatal, practices? Multiple criminological perspectives, including those described in prior chapters, could be applied to assist in understanding unnecessary medical procedures. One that seems to provide significant insight into the problem is Tittle's (1995, 2004) control balance theory as it emphasizes the amount of power doctors exercise when recommending surgery or tests, as well as highlights the inherent power differential between physicians and patients.

Control Balance Theory

Charles Tittle (1995) introduced his integrated theory of deviance as a means of accounting for a wide array of deviant or criminal behaviors, including white-collar offending. At the center of control balance theory is the concept of the control ratio. The control ratio refers to a comparison between the amount of power one is subjected to and the amount of power one can exert. A balanced control ratio means that the level of power one can exert over others and situations in his/her life is equal to the amount of power s/he experiences (Tittle, 1995, 2004). The control ratio is influenced by multiple factors including a person's social status and individual, as well as situational characteristics. According to Tittle (1995), individuals are more inclined to engage in deviance when their control ratio is unbalanced. He further argues that control imbalances motivate people to engage in crime/deviance because humans ultimately desire to be autonomous. In particular, this perspective distinguishes between control surpluses and control deficits, and explicates how each form of imbalance contributes to unique forms of deviance. A control surplus is present when a person can exercise more control than s/he is subject to, whereas a control deficit exists when one is subject to more control than s/he can exercise (Tittle, 1995).

All forms of control imbalance raise the likelihood of deviance, but as Tittle (1995) asserts, specific forms of deviance are associated with each type of imbalance. Control deficits are likely to result in acts of repressive deviance including submission, defiance, and predation. In comparison, control surpluses are associated with autonomous forms of deviance such as exploitation, plunder, and decadence (see Table 3.1 for a description of types of deviance). Although control imbalances are believed to increase the likelihood of offending, it does not mean that an imbalance will automatically result in deviant behavior. Control balance also integrates ideas from rational choice perspectives, as well as control theory to explain the

Table 3.1 Variations in the Control Ratio and Forms of Deviance

Control Deficit: Repressive Forms of Deviance

Submission	Instances where an individual engages in complete, passive obedience to others. The individual may allow him/herself to be taken advantage of or physically/sexually abused. This is somewhat similar to learned helplessness where an individual no longer tries to escape a violent or dangerous situation due to repeated exposure to violence.
Defiance	Situations where an individual engages in behavior that is in direct conflict with social expectations or norms in order to express contempt or dissatisfaction with a norm(s) or entity associated with respective societal ideals/norms. This may include acts like vandalism, substance abuse, participating in a worker strike, or a political protest.
Predation	Refers to direct forms of predation and may include theft, rape, homicide, robbery, assault, or fraud.

Control Balance

Conformity	Compliance with societal norms and expectations.

Control Surplus: Autonomous Forms of Deviance

Exploitation	Involves indirect forms of predation such as price-fixing, harassment via third parties, or benefitting from poor working conditions that endanger employees.
Plunder	Situations in which individuals or organizations disregard the needs or well-being of others in pursuit of their own interests. Examples include toxic waste dumping by corporations and genocide.
Decadence	Refers to impulsive behavior/actions guided by little rational thought and influenced by a life characterized by unconstrained indulgence. For instance, sadistic torture and group sex with children are grouped under this category.

Source: Tittle, C. R. (1995). *Control balance: Toward a general theory of deviance.* Boulder, CO: Westview Press.

underlying processes that link control imbalances to deviance. More specifically, the individual must recognize such an imbalance exists and per-
ceive that deviance will rectify it. Piquero and Hickman (1999) argue that
people may recognize the imbalance via "situational provocations" such as
a demotion, job termination, professional reprimand, or verbal affronts to
the individual's character (p. 323). Moreover, the opportunity to commit
deviance must exist in conjunction with an absence of constraint. In other
words, a person must be able to act on the motivation to commit deviance
without being bound by constraining forces such as fear of detection, sanction, or arrest.

Viewing unnecessary surgeries through the lens of control balance theory,
it seems that this behavior fits well within Tittle's (1995) notion of the control surplus, and more specifically, within his concept of plunder, considering that doctors who engage in this behavior do so with a blatant disregard
for the harms imposed on patients. Fiduciary relationships involving those
with autarchic power, such as the one between physicians and most patients,
render conditions that promote exploitation. In comparison, because street
criminals oftentimes experience financial strain while physicians and other
elite professionals enjoy large salaries, their motivation for deviance often
stems from greed (Braithwaite, 1997). As noted by Stahel et al. (2017),
one of the main reasons unnecessary procedures occur is the immense
incentives associated with surgical procedures (e.g., professional recognition, monetary gain, or both). Additionally, physicians function relatively
autonomously when prescribing a medical procedure despite the existence
of oversight mechanisms like state medical boards. By the virtue of "medical expertise," doctors have the ability to recommend procedures to patients
based on their professional opinions. Compared to most patients, physicians
procure more prestigious educational training, larger salaries, and higher
levels of respect, trust, and authority (Friedrichs, 2010). Ultimately, this culminates in the physician's ability to exert more control than s/he is subjected
to while simultaneously putting patients in the category of control deficit.
Patients may submit to the power of the physician due to the social status
and deference conferred to the profession and the vulnerability associated
with their status as patient.

All patients are susceptible to exploitation, however, those who deviate
from an "idealized empowered client" (i.e., healthy, educated, financially
stable) are most vulnerable (National Bioethics Advisory Commission,
2001). For example, in a case involving an ophthalmologist treating mentally ill residents of adult care homes in New York, it was discovered he
performed over 50 surgeries on 30 residents within an 18-month period. By
using methods nested in coercion and deceit, this physician targeted those
patients who were the most vulnerable (Levy, 2002). It was even discovered

that he created a ratings system for potential victims according to their level of vulnerability. Though this is an abridged explanation of Tittle's theory, cases such as this one demonstrate the nefarious nature of physician crime and depict the diminished ability of patients to protect themselves due to deficits of control.

Sexual Abuse by Doctors

> For me, the scariest night of my life happened when I was 15 years old. I had flown all day and night to get to Tokyo [for a competition]. [Nassar gave] me a sleeping pill for the flight, and the next thing I know, I was all alone with him in his hotel room getting a "treatment." I thought I was going to die that night. As it turns out . . . Dr. Nassar was not a doctor, he in fact is, was, and forever shall be, a child molester and a monster of a human being. End of story. He abused my trust, he abused my body and he left scars on my psyche that may never go away.
>
> (*The Guardian*, 2018, n.p.)

The quote above is an excerpt from Gold Medal Olympic gymnast McKayla Maroney's testimony at Larry Nassar's sentencing hearing and provides significant insight into the detrimental effects of sexual abuse by doctors. In general, sexual victimization refers to any unwanted sexual behavior and includes both contact (e.g., rape, sexual assault), as well as non-contact offenses (e.g., voyeurism, verbal sexual harassment, exposure) (Daigle, 2018). Within the context of health care, sexual victimization includes situations in which medical professionals engage in a variety of sexually abusive behaviors wherein the victim, in this case a patient, did not provide consent. The Federation of State Medical Boards (FSMB) (2006) outlines specific guidelines that address sexual misconduct by doctors and defines physician sexual misconduct as "behavior that exploits the physician-patient relationship in a sexual way (n.p.)." The FSMB guidelines elaborate that this behavior may be physical or verbal in nature and delineate between sexual impropriety and sexual violation. *Sexual impropriety* refers to "behaviors, gestures, or expressions" that are of a sexual nature, do not respect a patient's privacy, and/or are sexually degrading (FSMB, 2006, n.p.). Examples of sexual impropriety provided by the FSMB include, among others, watching a patient disrobe, performing a vaginal examination without gloves, discussing sexual fantasies or preferences with the patient, and using the doctor-patient relationship to acquire a date or sex.

In comparison, *sexual violations* are conceptualized as situations involving physical, sexual contact between the patient and the physician or other behavior that could be viewed as being sexual. According to the FSMB

(2006), this category of offenses includes any vaginal, oral, or anal intercourse or contact, as well as masturbation by a doctor in the presence of a patient (or vice versa). It also encompasses kissing, as well as the fondling (touching without a medically validated purpose) of breasts, genitals, or other sexualized body parts. Finally, another example of a sexual violation would be the exchange of sex or sexual behaviors for prescription drugs and other medically related procedures/practices.

A recent series of articles entitled "Doctors & Sex Abuse" published in the *Atlanta Journal Constitution* (AJC) sought to draw attention to sex abuse by doctors and provides numerous examples of this type of behavior (see Ernsthausen, 2016; Hart & Teegardin, 2016; Teegardin, Robbins, Ernsthausen, & Hart, 2016). The cases cited throughout the articles illustrate how the two forms of sexual misconduct identified by the FSMB, impropriety and violations, typically co-occur. Consider the following cases drawn from the AJC's series:

- A doctor in Illinois had his license suspended in 2014 for sexual misconduct. One of his patients filed a law suit alleging that he felt her breast and when she protested he "leaned back and briefly masturbated while smiling at her."
 (Hart & Teegardin, 2016, n.p.)

- According to the state medical board in New Mexico, an ear, nose, and throat doctor completed genital exams on anesthetized patients. The doctor claimed the exams were for screening purposes. These patients had not consented to a genital examination.
 (Teegardin et al., 2016)

- A doctor in Kentucky was accused of placing his hand down a patient's blouse, removing her breast and placing "his mouth on it." He then reportedly proceeded to expose his genitals to her and "ejaculated on her hand."
 (Teegardin et al., 2016, n.p.)

- A doctor in Maine was reported by fellow employees for having naked photographs of females at his desk and inappropriately touching patients. Nurses also reported that he had examined the "rectal and vaginal area" of an anesthetized female patient prior to a surgical procedure without wearing gloves.
 (Ernsthausen, 2016, n.p.)

It is difficult to determine the true extent of sexual misconduct by doctors and diverse estimates are presented in the literature. The prevalence figures provided in the literature are based on self-reports, both victim and perpetrator, or cases reported to medical boards or other authorities. Thus, they provide an incomplete picture at best and, arguably, can be considered conservative estimates. An early study by Dehlendrof and Wolfe (1998) used data derived from disciplinary action reports submitted by state medical boards and federal agencies between 1989 and 1996. In the final year of the study period, they found that right under 5% of disciplinary orders were for sex-related offenses, just below the 5.2% peak in 1994. Three-fourths of the cases examined by these two scholars involved patients as victims. Grant and Alfred (2007) established that approximately 7% of sanctions between 1994 and 2002 reported in the FSMB Data Center were for sexual misconduct. In a more recent study based on public-use data from the National Practitioner Data Bank (NPDB) for the years 2003 to 2013, AbuDagga, Wolfe, Carome, and Oshel (2016) found that 1,039 physicians had reports of sexual misconduct in the database. These physicians comprised roughly 1% of all physicians who had any kind of report in the NPDB (AbuDagga et al., 2016). Like sexual victimization more broadly, it is believed that underreporting is pervasive. In fact, Tillinghast and Cournos (2000) estimate that less than 5% of victims report physician/patient sexual contact.

In addition to identifying rates of sexual misconduct by doctors, scholars have uncovered specific trends in offending. As evidenced in the Nassar case, some research suggests that doctors who engage in sexual abuse of patients are chronic, repeat offenders (Tillinghast & Cournos, 2000). AbuDagga and colleagues (2016) found that nearly 13% of the doctors with sexual misconduct reports in their sample were multiple offenders. Moreover, research by DuBois and colleagues (2017) indicates that sexually abusive physicians engage in a wide variety of abusive behaviors and often perpetrate multiple forms of abuse. Examining 101 cases of sexual misconduct, they found that most cases involved inappropriate touching (33%) followed by sodomy (31%). 16% of the cases in their sample were classified as rape and 14% were identified as child molestation (DuBois et al., 2017). Their analysis further revealed evidence that physicians who sexually abused patients do not generally specialize in one form of deviance, rather they seem to engage in multiple types of misbehavior. For instance, they found that doctors who molested children were significantly more likely to engage in other forms of sexual misconduct against their patients (e.g., voyeurism) relative to doctors who committed other forms of sexual abuse. Additionally, research has found that most victims are female (AbuDagga et al., 2016; DuBois et al., 2017) and the majority of physicians who sexually abuse patients are male (DuBois et al., 2017). Sexually abusive physicians also tend to be older than the general physician population (AbuDagga et al., 2016). Looking further at physician characteristics, studies based on data from state medical boards suggest that psychiatrists, family/general medical practitioners, and OBG-YNs are most often represented among doctors who are sanctioned for sexual misconduct (Dehlendrof & Wolfe, 1998; Sansone & Sansone, 2009; Tillinghast & Cournos, 2000).

Under FSMB guidelines and American Medical Association (AMA) ethical codes, *sexual contact or a sexual relationship between a consenting patient and a physician* can also be considered abuse. The AMA states that romantic/sexual interactions between doctors and patients "may exploit the vulnerability of the patient, compromise the physician's ability to make objective judgments about the patient's health care, and ultimately be detrimental to the patient's well-being" (AMA, 2018, n.p.). A key factor to consider when examining romantic or sexual relationships between a doctor and a patient is the notion of consent. Based on their expertise and authority as medical professionals, doctors hold intrinsic power over their patients. Their role affords them the ability to guide behavior and change lives through their advice, the prescription of medication, and the use of medical procedures. This, coupled with the prestige assigned to the medical profession, may create an environment conducive to coercion and manipulation of the physician-patient relationship.

Acknowledging the power differential inherent in doctor-patient relationships, the AMA has officially stated in a written opinion based on their foundational principles—AMA Principles of Medical Ethics I, II, and IV—that consensual romantic and sexual relationships between current patients and their doctors are, in essence, prohibited. If doctors want to pursue a romantic or sexual relationship with a patient, the AMA (2018) advises that they should no longer oversee the patient's medical care and discontinue the doctor-patient relationship. However, even in this case, since the power dynamics inherent in the prior relationship may spill over into the current situation and lead to a coercive, and possibly exploitative environment, the AMA (2018) ethical guidelines urge caution and discourage such relationships. It is difficult, if not impossible, to estimate the extent of consensual relationships between doctors and their patients because much of the research in this area focuses on nonconsensual sexual contact. Not to mention, as previously noted, much of this behavior goes unreported by victims. A study by DuBois and colleagues (2017), for instance, found that 7% of sampled cases involved consensual sex between a patient and doctor.

Explaining Sexual Violence by Doctors Against Patients

To understand sexual misconduct, we draw upon rational choice perspectives within the field of criminology. This group of theories can be found in a number of disciplines and form the basis of classical criminological thought. Rational choice and deterrence theories can be traced back to the work of scholars like Hobbes, Beccaria, and Bentham.

Rational choice and deterrence perspectives highlight the decision-making process that underlies offending and suggest that humans are naturally self-interested. And as such they are inclined to behave in ways that advance their own interests. The fundamental premise is rooted in Bentham's concept of hedonistic calculus that posits that potential offenders rationally weigh the costs and benefits of criminal behavior when deciding whether to engage in crime (Kubrin, Stucky, & Krohn, 2009). Based on this notion of a rational "hedonistic calculus," offenders are more likely to engage in crime when the perceived costs or consequences of crime are low, and the potential benefits are believed to be high. Consequences can involve formal sanctions (e.g., arrest) or can come from informal sources (e.g., parental disappointment, loss of friends), and are conceptualized as a likely deterrent to potential offenders if they are perceived to be severe, certain, and swiftly applied.

Modern rational choice theories have attempted to respond to some of the critiques of early iterations by more thoroughly outlining the target/victim selection process, describing the importance of opportunity, and clarifying the role of "rationality" in offender decision-making (for more thorough discussions of the evolution and critiques of rational choice theory, see Clarke & Cornish, 2001; Kubrin et al., 2009). We have already discussed one modern theory rooted in the rational choice framework with our application of Cohen and Felson's (1979) routine activities theory to fraud by physicians. Cohen and Felson (1979) argue that it is important to understand why one target is selected over another and do not attempt to do so through explaining offender motivation which is a constant by their account. They focus on criminal opportunities and suggest that targets are selected based on the presence of three components: 1) a motivated offender, 2) suitable target, and 3) capable guardianship. To briefly restate the chief argument, routine activities theory posits that crime is more likely to occur when a suitable target and motivated offender converge in time and space in the absence of capable guardianship (Cohen & Felson, 1979). As originally articulated, Cohen and Felson (1979) proposed this theory as a mechanism for understanding "direct-contact predatory" offenses, however, as previously discussed in *Chapter 2*, subsequent applications have extended the theoretical framework to a wide array of crimes such as drug dealing and fraud (Felson, 2001).

Rational choice more broadly, and routine activities theory more specifically, are fruitful frameworks for understanding sexual abuse by doctors. First, sexual abuse fits clearly within the original domain of routine activities theory as it is a direct-contact predatory offense. The literature also suggests that the consequences for sexual misconduct are substantially low. As previously discussed, only a small percentage of victims report their victimization to authorities, thus the likelihood of detection is low. This leads motivated offenders, in this case physicians, to view patients as suitable targets in that they are not likely to report the victimization to authorities. Further, an examination of the research based on formal sanctions by state medical boards indicates that the penalties for doctors who are reported are relatively mild and that many physicians continue to practice medicine after engaging in sexual misconduct (AbuDagga et al., 2016). This does little in terms of deterrence and contributes to a lack of capable guardianship in that sanctioned physicians can reenter the medical professional to pick up their patterns of behavior without any meaningful incentive to desist. This leaves patients vulnerable to victimization, and in some cases revictimization.

Further elaborating on the concept of guardianship and target suitability, many cases of sexual misconduct occur in an exam room where the only people in the room are the physician and the patient (DuBois et al., 2017). In some cases, such as those involving inappropriate touching, a patient may not even realize that misconduct occurred. For instance, consider cases where doctors have removed their gloves during vaginal exams or sexually abused the patient while s/he was anesthetized or sedated. Anesthetized patients could be considered to epitomize the construct of a suitable target in that they are unable to resist the offender, and some may be completely unaware that the victimization occurred because they were unconscious. Norder (2016) discusses the cases of five different doctors who assaulted patients while they were under anesthesia, with several doctors accused of masturbating on sedated patients. She describes a victim in Texas who woke up from a colonoscopy to see her physician's penis and someone wiping off her mouth and cheek. The patient requested police perform a mouth swab and sperm was found (Norder, 2016). Had this patient not awoken, she may have never realized she was victimized.

Conclusion

Physical abuse by doctors in the form of unnecessary procedures and sexual victimization comprise a unique form of deviance by doctors. These behaviors are distinct in terms of their invasive nature and the impact these violations have on patients. As demonstrated throughout this chapter, unnecessary surgeries can result in substantial economic consequences to patients in terms of the cost associated with medical procedures. Moreover, these interventions have the potential to take a physical toll on the patient, including the possibility of permanent disability or even death in some cases. Similarly, sexual abuse may affect a patient across his/her lifetime. Studies of sexual violence more broadly suggest that victims may experience a multitude of mental health problems such as PTSD, depression, anxiety, and suicidal ideation (Daigle, 2018). The existing literature suggests the current environment of the medical field, which is characterized by a lack of oversight, weak sanctions for misbehavior, and the high level of trust and prestige afforded to medical providers, contribute to physical abuse and sexual offending by doctors. The two criminological perspectives, control balance theory and the rational choice perspective, presented in the current chapter provide some insight into the underlying processes that influence the nature of physical abuse committed by doctors.

Notes

1. Mirroring the literature, throughout this chapter the phrase "unnecessary procedures" is used to describe a broad range of medical services, including X-rays and cesarean deliveries that are not medically necessary.
2. Iatrogenic is a medical term referring to a physical or mental condition caused by a physician or health care provider (e.g., iatrogenic disease) due to exposure to pathogens, toxins, or injurious treatment or procedures (McGraw-Hill, 2002).
3. Deaths due to iatrogenesis are responsible for over 225,000 deaths annually in the U.S. (Bleakley, 2014).
4. Since only 26 procedures were examined in the study, it is likely that the rate of patient exposure to unnecessary medical practices is much higher than reported (Welch et al., 2012).

References

AbuDagga, A., Wolfe, S. M., Carome, M., & Oshel, R. E. (2016). Cross-sectional analysis of the 1039 US physicians reported to the National Practitioner Data Bank for sexual misconduct, 2003–2013. *PLoS One, 11*(2), 1–13.

Adams, D. (2018, May 24). Victims share what Larry Nassar did to them under the guise of medical treatment. *The Indy Star.* Retrieved from www.indystar.com/story/news/2018/01/25/heres-what-larry-nassar-actually-did-his-patients/1065165001/

Al-Khatib, S. M., Hellkamp, A., Curtis, J., Mark, D., Peterson, E., Sanders, G. D., . . . Hammill, S. (2011). Non-evidence-based ICD implantations in the United States. *JAMA, 305*(1), 43–49.

American Medical Association. (2018). *Code of medical ethics opinion 9.1.1.* Retrieved from www.ama-assn.org/delivering-care/romantic-or-sexual-relationships-patients

Arora, K. S., Douglas, S., & Goold, S. D. (2014). What brings physicians to disciplinary review? A further subcategorization. *AJOB Empirical Bioethics, 5*(4), 53–60.

Bernstein, S. J. (2000). The appropriateness of recommendations for hysterectomy. *American College of Obstetricians and Gynecologists, 95,* 199–205.

Bleakley, A. (2014). Communication hypocompetence: An iatrogenic epidemic. In *Patient-centered medicine in transition* (pp. 21–29). Springer International Publishing.

Braithwaite, J. (1997). Charles Tittle's control balance and criminological theory. *Theoretical Criminology, 1*(1), 77–97.

Clarke, R. V., & Cornish, D. B. (2001). Rational choice. In R. Paternoster & R. Bachman (Eds.), *Explaining criminals and crime* (pp. 23–42). New York, NY: Oxford University Press.

Cohen, L. E., & Felson, M. (1979). Social change and crime rate trends: A routine activities approach. *American Sociological Review, 44*(4), 588–608.

Daigle, L. (2018). *Victimology: The essentials* (2nd ed.). Thousand Oaks, CA: Sage Publications.

Dehlendrof, C. E., & Wolfe, S. E. (1998). Physicians disciplined for sex-related offenses. *JAMA, 279*(23), 1883–1888.

DuBois, J. M., Walsh, H. A., Chibnall, J. T., Anderson, E. E., Eggers, M. R., Fowose, M., & Ziobrowski, H. (2017). Sexual violation of patients by physicians: A mixed-methods, exploratory analysis of 101 cases. *Journal of Interpersonal Violence*, 1–21. doi:10.1177/1079063217712217

Eappen, S., Lane, B. H., Rosenberg, B., Lipsitz, S. A., Sadoff, D., Matheson, D., . . . Gawande, A. A. (2013). Relationship between occurrence of surgical complications and hospital finances. *JAMA, 309*(15), 1599–1606.

Ernsthausen, J. (2016, July 6). Dangerous doctors, flawed data. *The Atlanta Journal Constitution.* Retrieved from http://doctors.ajc.com/sex_abuse_national_database/?ecmp=doctorssexabuse_microsite_nav

Federation of State Medical Boards. (2006). *Addressing sexual boundaries: Guidelines for state medical boards.* Washington, DC: Federation of State Medical Boards.

Felson, M. (2001). The routine activities approach: A very versatile theory of crime. In R. Paternoster & R. Bachman (Eds.), *Explaining criminals and crime* (pp. 43–46). New York, NY: Oxford University Press.

Friedrichs, D. O. (2010). *Trusted criminals: White collar crime in contemporary society.* Belmont, CA: Wadsworth.

Grant, D., & Alfred, K. C. (2007). Sanctions and recidivism: An evaluation of physician discipline by state medical boards. *Journal of Health Politics, Policy, and Law, 32*(5), 867–885.

The Guardian. (2018). Victim impact statements against Larry Nassar: "I thought I was going to die." Retrieved from www.theguardian.com/sport/2018/jan/24/victim-impact-statements-against-larry-nassar-i-thought-i-was-going-to-die

Hart, A., & Teegardin, C. (2016). Hurt that doesn't heal. *The Atlanta Journal Constitution.* Retrieved from http://doctors.ajc.com/patient_stories_sexual_abuse_doctors/?ecmp=doctorssexabuse_microsite_stories

Hogan, S. (2016). Medical crime: Occupational crime at its worst. *Sociological Imagination: Western's Undergraduate Sociology Student Journal, 5*(1), 5.

Jesilow, P., Pontell, H. N., & Geis, G. (1985). Medical criminals: Physicians and white-collar offenses. *Justice Quarterly, 2*, 149–165.

Kelley, R. (2009). *Where can $700 billion in waste be cut annually from the US healthcare system.* Ann Arbor, MI: Thomson Reuters.

Kozhimannil, K. B., Law, M. R., & Virnig, B. A. (2013). Cesarean delivery rates vary tenfold among US hospitals; reducing variation may address quality and cost issues. *Health Affairs, 32*(3), 527–535.

Kubrin, C. E., Stucky, T. D., & Krohn, M. D. (2009). *Researching theories of crime and deviance*. New York, NY: Oxford University Press.

Leape, L. L. (1989). Unnecessary surgery. *Health Services Research, 24*(3), 351.

Leape, L. L. (2015a). Hospital readmissions following surgery: Turning complications into "treasures." *JAMA, 313*(5), 467–468.

Leape, L. L. (2015b). Patient safety in the era of healthcare reform. *Clinical Orthopaedics and Related Research, 473*(5), 1568–1573.

Levinson, W., Kallewaard, M., Bhatia, R. S., Wolfson, D., Shortt, S., & Kerr, E. A. (2015). "Choosing Wisely": A growing international campaign. *BMJ Qual Saf, 24*(2), 167–174.

Levy, C. J. (2002, April 28). For mentally ill, death and misery. *New York Times*. Retrieved from www.nytimes.com/2002/04/28/nyregion/for-mentally-ill-death-and-misery.html

Lyu, H., Xu, T., Brotman, D., Mayer-Blackwell, B., Cooper, M., Daniel, M., Wick, E. C., Saini, V., Brownlee, S., & Makary, M. A. (2017). Overtreatment in the United States. *PLoS One, 12*(9), 1–11.

McGraw-Hill. (2002). *Concise dictionary of modern medicine*. New York: McGraw-Hill.

Mehta, J., Tribble, L., & Mehta, J. L. (2011). Healthcare in the United States: Unnecessary procedures, lawsuits, and skyrocketing costs. *Journal of Forensic Research Sciences, 2*(2), 1–2.

National Bioethics Advisory Commission. (2001). *Ethical and policy issues in research involving human participants*. Bethesda, MD: National Bioethics Advisory Commission.

Norder, L. (2016, August 2). 5 doctors who abused sedated patients. *The Atlanta Journal Constitution*. Retrieved from http://doctors.ajc.com/doctor_sex_abuse_sedated/

Oberlander, J., & Laugesen, M. J. (2015). Leap of faith: Medicare's new physician payment system. *New England Journal of Medicine, 373*(13), 1185–1187.

Piquero, A. R., & Hickman, M. (1999). An empirical test of Tittle's control balance theory. *Criminology, 37*(2), 319–342.

Sansone, R. A., & Sansone, L. A. (2009). Crossing the line: Sexual boundary violations by physicians. *Psychiatry, 6*(6), 45–48.

Singh, H., Giardina, T. D., Meyer, A. N., Forjuoh, S. N., Reis, M. D., & Thomas, E. J. (2013). Types and origins of diagnostic errors in primary care settings. *JAMA, 173*(6), 418–425.

Smith, M., Saunders, R., Stuckhardt, L., & McGinnis, J. M. (2013). *Best care at lower cost: The path to continuously learning health care in America*. Washington, DC: National Academies Press.

Stahel, P. F., VanderHeiden, T. F., & Kim, F. J. (2017). Why do surgeons continue to perform unnecessary surgery? *Patient Safety in Surgery, 11*(1), 1–2.

Teegardin, C., Robbins, D., Ernsthausen, J., & Hart, A. (2016, July 6). License to betray. *The Atlanta Journal Constitution*. Retrieved from http://doctors.ajc.com/part_1_license_to_betray/

Tillinghast, E., & Cournos, F. (2000). Assessing the risk of recidivism in physicians with histories of sexual misconduct. *Journal of Forensic Sciences, 45*(6), 1184–1189.

Tittle, C. R. (1995). *Control balance: Toward a general theory of deviance.* Boulder, CO: Westview Press.

Tittle, C. R. (2004). Refining control balance theory. *Theoretical Criminology, 8*(4), 395–428.

U. S. Department of Health and Human Services. (2014). *Health care fraud and abuse control program annual report.* Retrieved from http://oig.hhs.gov/publications/docs/hcfac/FY2014-hcfac.pdf

U. S. Department of Health and Human Services. (2015). *Health care fraud and abuse control program annual report.* Retrieved from http://oig.hhs.gov/publications/docs/hcfac/FY2015-hcfac.pdf

Welch, H. G., Hayes, K. J., & Frost, C. (2012). Repeat testing among Medicare beneficiaries. *Archives of Internal Medicine, 172*(22), 1745–1751.

4   Responding to Crime and Deviance by Physicians

Over the years, health care expenditures in the U.S. have grown inexorably, raising concerns that costs are spiraling out of control. As the most expensive system globally, our government spends nearly double the amount for health care as other high-income nations such as England, Denmark, and Japan (Papanicolas et al., 2018). Compared to 1960 when approximately 5% of the nation's gross domestic product (GDP) went toward national health care expenditures (Garner & McCabe, 2012), federal allocations for medical care currently constitute roughly one-fifth of the GDP (McPeak, 2018). With forecasts of continued increases in costs, our economy may not be able to withstand this escalating financial burden. Attesting to this, some experts warn of an impending Medicare program collapse that could jeopardize the health and lives of millions of Americans (Roy, 2011). In this regard, few challenges loom larger for policymakers and law enforcement.

Sound fiscal management of our nation's health care system depends on how well authorities can identify and mitigate the factors underpinning the expenditure uptrend. Among other contributors (e.g., excessive administrative costs, an aging population, and increased hospitalizations), the financial and operational structure of America's public health care programs is prime for exploitation. In particular, the rising tide of health care fraud has been chiefly attributed to the current pay-and-chase payment model (Roy, 2011). Under this reimbursement framework, the lack of pre-authorization safeguards, paired with low surveillance, allows fraudulent invoices to be easily submitted and paid (Pontell, Jesilow, & Geis, 1982; Roy, 2011). Thus, presenting deceitful actors with ample opportunities to fleece programs like Medicare and Medicaid without much concern for detection. In response, the federal government has tried to stem this tide through statutory, regulatory, and technological innovations. As will be evident in the discussion below, much of the focus on misconduct has centered on the response to fraud by physicians as opposed to violence by doctors. Notably falling in the fringes of political and public discourse is sexual misconduct at the hands of trusted physicians, however, the rise of the #MeToo movement may begin to remedy this oversight.

In the sections that follow, we take a closer look at fraud control efforts, as well as note some of the measures in place to address sexual misconduct. Moreover, we will highlight some of the challenges encountered in the pursuit of health care fraud convictions and the response to sexual misconduct complaints. We open with a discussion of advancements in health care law, which solely targets fraudulent behaviors. Attention is then given to government enforcement and regulatory actions taken against physician fraud and abuse/violence. We close by highlighting the legal complexities associated with these cases, including problems with establishing proof that a crime occurred and the role of victims in the criminal justice process.

Statutory Responses to Medical Deviance

The 1863 Civil False Claims Act (FCA)—a relic of the Civil War, along with its signature whistleblowing exemptions—has long served as the principal legal tool for defending public programs from corruptive practices (Sparrow, 2008). Violators of the FCA only incur civil penalties, however. Signifying the growing recognition of health care fraud's seriousness among politicians and government officials, Capitol Hill lawmakers have since then passed narrower statutes aimed at deviant medical practices. These new laws articulate guidelines for prosecuting dishonest health care providers, giving authorities greater leverage in the fight against medical crimes. Of these, the most prominent statutes include the Anti-Kickback Statute, the Health Insurance Portability and Accountability Act, and the Patient Protection and Affordable Care Act.

We first turn our attention to the 1972 Anti-Kickback Statute (AKS). AKS prohibits health care providers from deliberately paying or receiving remuneration that might entice referrals for services payable by federal and state-run health care programs (Office of the Inspector General, 2017). Regardless of the actual medical necessity of the referral, doing so is deemed a felony that carries a maximum sentence of five years in prison (Leap, 2011). Indeed, some industries permit such incentives. But in the medical sphere, aside from imprisonment, culprits who violate this law also face fines of up to three times the kickback amount (plus $50,000.00 per kickback), revocation of medical licensure, and exclusion from coverage networks (Mannava, Bercovitch, & Grant-Kels, 2013). Because the broad prohibitive provisions of AKS could entangle some legitimate business arrangements, "safe harbor" exceptions were later included to protect enterprises that would otherwise be subject to criminal prosecution (see Morrison, 2000 for a full discussion of AKS).[1]

The next major U.S. health care-related law was enacted nearly a quarter century after the passage of AKS. The Health Insurance Portability and Accountability Act (HIPAA), most famous for its protections of patients' health care information and access rights, was crafted to curtail health care waste, fraud, and abuse. HIPAA provisions not only broadened the prosecution of health care fraud but also appropriated monies to several fraud control efforts, namely the Health Care Fraud and Abuse Control Program (HCFAC). This anti-fraud initiative remains a critical funding source for agencies tasked with tackling health care crimes against public insurers, including the Office of the Inspector General (OIG) and Justice Department (DOJ) (Blank, Kasprisin, & White, 2009). Under the joint direction of the U.S. Attorney General's Office and the Secretary of the Department of Health and Human Services (HHS), HCFAC collaborations with federal, state, and local law enforcement have successfully brought down numerous fraud schemes since its inception (Sullivan, 2018). In 2017 alone, these collaborative efforts led to 639 convictions and over $2.6 billion in recoveries, much of which came from criminal fines and civil settlements related to Medicare losses (U.S. HHS, 2018a).

The most recent statutory innovation, the Patient Protection and Affordable Care Act (ACA), went into effect in 2010. Popularly known as Obamacare, the ACA was developed to enhance the quality and cost-effectiveness of the public health care system. With over 2,400 pages of new law, the ACA contains several preventative and proactive measures for reducing fraudulent activities within both Medicare and Medicaid (Gable, 2011). Intended to strengthen and beef up anti-fraud efforts, this Obama-era bill has allocated upwards of $350 million toward fraud-fighting efforts since its rollout (e.g., predictive modeling technologies). It also established more stringent screening protocols, as well as stiffer civil and criminal penalties for health care crimes (Office of the Inspector General, 2017). Without question, the passage of the ACA brought about lasting changes in health care fraud enforcement. Since 2010, the number of individuals brought forward on charges of health care fraud has increased by 75% (Office of the Inspector General, 2017).[2]

Enforcement of Anti–Health Care Fraud and Abuse Laws in the U.S.

In addition to the legislative solutions described above, the U.S. government has targeted deviant medical providers in response to the problem of health care fraud and abuse. While the FBI is recognized as the primary investigative agency for crimes in both the private and public sectors (Morris, 2009), lawmakers have created several regulatory agencies to handle misconduct in health care. With an arsenal of federal statutes at its disposal, our government pursues the prosecution of health care offenders through several legal and administrative avenues.

Medicaid Fraud Control Units

Both the federal and state government agendas against health care fraud officially began following special prosecutor Charles J. Hynes' congressional testimony in 1976. Well known for his groundbreaking investigation of fraud in New York's nursing home industry, Hynes strongly encouraged Congress to institute a fraud control unit in each state. Heeding Hynes' call, President Carter signed the Medicare-Medicaid Anti-Fraud and Abuse Amendments into law a year later, establishing Medicaid fraud units in every state (Nokes, 2016). Remarkably, up to that point, no federal or state agency was tasked with investigating fraud and crime within public health care programs. Nor were any meaningful preventative controls in place.

Composed mainly of investigators, auditors, and attorneys, Medicaid Fraud Control Units (MFCUs) are state entities charged with investigating Medicaid fraud. Although participation was initially voluntary, as of 1995, federal law mandates that each state maintain an MFCU unless "the operation of a unit would not be cost-effective because minimal Medicaid fraud exists in a particular state and the state has other adequate safeguards to protect beneficiaries from abuse or neglect" (U.S. HHS, 2018b, p. 1). With the exception of North Dakota, MFCUs are currently staffed in every state, as well as the District of Columbia.

Created to focus solely on Medicaid fraud, the jurisdictional authority of these units was extended with the enactment of the Ticket to Work and Work Incentives Improvement Act in 1999. Now authorized to investigate and prosecute (with the approval of the Inspector General) similar crimes in other federally funded health care programs, MFCUs have obtained prosecutions in nearly every segment of the health care enterprise, including nursing homes, hospitals, *medical equipment* companies, and pharmacies. The following cases illustrate the diverse array of schemes sought out by MFCUs:

- In September of 2015, collaborations between the Florida MFCU and local police led to the arrest and conviction of a dentist for her part in phantom and doubling billing schemes. Months later, she was sentenced to three years of community supervision and ordered to pay back $120,000. This oral care professional also loss her dentistry license and is prohibited from ever practicing again.

(Agency for Healthcare Administration, 2016)

- In a highly publicized New York case, a Long Island pharmacist was convicted for spearheading a large-scale drug diversion scam. According to Attorney General Eric Schneiderman, the lead defendant brokered the sale of black-market HIV medications from 2008 to 2012, netting him roughly $25 million in illegal profits. These unlawfully obtained drugs were repackaged and dispensed to Medicaid recipients via an online pharmacy. Further duping the system, his accomplices then falsely billed Medicaid nearly a quarter-billion-dollars for the diverted medications. In the end, he was stripped of his license, forced to pay restitution, and must serve between eight to 24 years in state prison.

  (New York State Attorney General's Office, 2019)

- Last year, a New Jersey doctor and a New York pediatrician confessed to taking kickbacks in exchange for referrals of patient blood specimen tests to Biodiagnostic Laboratory Services (BLS). Court documents revealed that both physicians were paid a flat fee of $3,000 per month plus additional cash based on the number of referrals. The doctor from New Jersey was sentenced to two years of supervised release and fined $4,000, while a U.S. District judge ordered his codefendant to serve one year of probation and fined him $75,000.

  (DOJ, 2018c)

Medicare Strike Force

One of the government's primary health care enforcement initiatives is the Medicare Fraud Strike Force. As the name implies, the central goal of this task force is detecting and prosecuting fraud against Medicare—the backbone of the U.S. health care system. Implemented by the DOJ and HHS to rein in health care system corruption, the Strike Force unifies the efforts of the DOJ, OIG, and Offices of the United States Attorneys. In collaboration with federal and local law enforcement, the Strike Force seeks to bring the most egregious and chronic health care fraud offenders to justice. This interagency task force identifies geographic "hot spots" or jurisdictions with high levels of suspicious billing activity. To keep up with the new era of digital transactions in health care, using state-of-the-art data analytics, similar to how credit card companies track and flag questionable purchases, investigators search for billing anomalies linked to health care fraud in real time (CMS, 2017).

First launched twelve years ago in South Florida, the Strike Force had an almost immediate impact. Barely a month after operations commenced, over 50 defendants were indicted for Medicare fraud involving pharmaceuticals

and therapy services (Morris, 2009). Now rebranded as Health Care Fraud
Prevention and Enforcement Action Team (HEAT), the Strike Force has
expanded its operations to ten additional hotspot locations: Los Angeles,
California; Tampa, Florida; Chicago, Illinois; Southern Louisiana; Detroit,
Michigan; Newark, New Jersey; Brooklyn, New York; Philadelphia, Penn-
sylvania; and Dallas and Houston, Texas (DOJ, 2018d). Since 2007, HEAT
teams have conducted 1,938 criminal investigations, indicted nearly 2,500
individuals, and successfully recovered about $3 billion stolen by white-
collars (U.S. HHS, 2018b). Below, we offer a couple of examples of HEAT's
recent enforcement actions:

• In a 2018 case, two doctors practicing in Dallas, Texas, along with
  several nurses, were sentenced for their involvement in an $11 million
  false claims scheme. For nearly eight years, this group of Texas-based
  offenders falsified nursing assessments, fabricated invoices for home
  health services never rendered, improperly certified Medicare beneficiaries, and billed for unnecessary services. Collectively, the five defendants were ordered to serve a total of 252 months in prison.

  (DOJ, 2018a)

• That same year, HEAT teams successfully pursued the conviction of
  a Detroit-area doctor, who along with her co-defendants, defrauded
  Medicare of just under $9 million through illegal health care kickbacks
  and fake billing claims. For her role in this five-year-long scheme, the
  defendant, who was not a licensed physician at the time, was sentenced
  to 135 months in prison.

  (DOJ, 2018b)

State Medical Boards

While law enforcement partnerships provide defense from exploitative health
care actions, they do not bear the full responsibility of maintaining quality
medical services. That designation belongs to state medical boards (SMB).
Authorized under the 10th Amendment of the U.S. Constitution (Federation of State Medical Boards, 2019), SMBs work to preserve the health,
safety, and overall welfare of the public. State boards govern physician practices through peer review, malpractice investigations, physician profiling,
and corrective actions. In comparison to MFCUs and strike forces, SMBs
are one of the main entities charged with responding to complaints of sexual
misconduct by physicians. Although primarily responsible for the licensing
and discipline of physicians, in many jurisdictions, other health care professionals fall under their control. For those doctors found to be in breach

of medical professional standards and ethical provisions, the board could impose public reprimands, fines, suspensions, or even revoke their physician's license (Federation of State Medical Boards, 2019). Historically, state boards have been run by licensed physicians. At first blush, this makes sense. Who better to govern medical practitioners than those with the necessary expertise and first-hand insight? This was the key premise behind the original makeup of these boards. Under this self-governed regime, however, doctors were rarely punished through formal means (Johnson & Chaudhry, 2012). Derailed by strong in-group loyalty, doctors often stuck together and resisted passing judgment on their peers (Leape, 1992; Sparrow, 2008). Similar to the blue code of silence in law enforcement, physicians still tend not to report dishonest colleagues. "Even when a physician or other provider is convicted of outright criminal fraud, and even when their actions have had profound adverse consequences for patients' health," Sparrow (2008, p. 1166) notes that, "their professional associations scarcely ever speak out against their conduct." This professional cohesion largely explains why doctors have failed to police themselves effectively.

As time passed, largely due to the front-page allegations of medical deviance, it became evident that clinicians required vigilant regulation and impartial oversight. During the mid-1980s, consumers began taking notice of state board decisions and demanded increased transparency and accountability. Boards now typically consist of volunteer clinicians and state-appointed civilian or non-physician members. In every state and U.S. territory, as well as the District of Columbia, a state board is responsible for establishing and enforcing laws and regulations aimed at defending against unprofessional, incompetent, or illegal conduct (Federation of State Medical Boards, 2019).

Critics allege that SMBs should do more to protect consumers from medical misconduct (see Fauber & Wynn, 2018). And perhaps with good reason. Looking at sexual misconduct specifically, doctors regularly receive a proverbial slap on the wrist by medical boards. Oftentimes this involves mandatory patient/doctor "boundary" counseling/therapy sessions before the doctor returns to practice (AbuDagga et al., 2016; Carr, 2003; Teegardin et al., 2016). Teegardin and colleagues (2016) found that the rationale behind such lenient sanctions was that doctors are just too valuable to remove from the field. For example, an executive director of the Alabama Board of Medical Examiners was quoted saying, " . . . the resources that have been poured into that doctor almost demand that you try to salvage that physician—if it's possible . . . (n.p.)." While many of the criticisms of SMBs are warranted (see, e.g., Eisler & Hansen, 2013; Teegardin et al., 2016), it is hard to refute the change in the regulatory climate since the inclusion of public board members. Illustrating a renewed commitment to patient safety, the yearly totals for doctors disciplined by SMBs have ballooned (Grant &

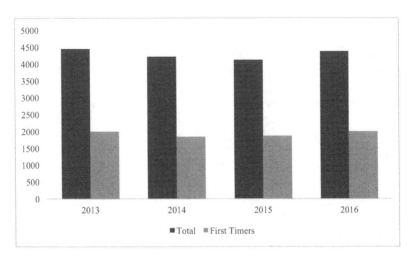

Figure 4.1 Number of U.S. Physicians with a Board Sanction by Year
Source: Federation of State Medical Boards, 2018

Alfred, 2007), with rates holding steady over the past decade. According to the *U.S. Medical Regulatory Trends and Actions Report*, 40% of the 4,081 physicians disciplined by state medical boards in 2017 were either placed on probation or had their license suspended or revoked. Appallingly, every year, more than half of the doctors sanctioned are repeat offenders (see Figure 4.1) (Federation of State Medical Boards, 2019).

In line with the shift toward greater transparency, medical boards publish information about doctors licensed in their state (e.g., disciplinary orders or actions by regulatory boards or agencies, suspensions or revocations of practicing privileges, criminal convictions, malpractice dispositions, and credentials). In addition, the Federation of State Medical Boards (FSMB)—a national nonprofit composed of licensing boards across the U.S.—has made its national database on physician licensure and disciplinary information, *DocInfo*, publicly available. Now granted the same access as SMBs and various other health care entities, citizens can look up a physician's license and discipline history. Researchers, however, have highlighted the limitations of such data, noting that categories linked to sanctions are often vague and provide little insight into why a doctor was sanctioned. For instance, Grant and Alfred (2007) found the codes "not applicable" and "unprofessional conduct" were often cited as a basis for a sanction. They assert that "not applicable" is assigned when a board and physician settle on a sanction that does not require the case disposition to be made public. "Unprofessional conduct" describes a wide array of behaviors ranging from inadequate record keeping to physical abuse of patients (Grant & Alfred, 2007). Several watchdog groups also provide information on state board disciplinary actions. One such group, Private Citizen, a nonpartisan organization, collects data and analyzes patterns of physician sanctioning for serious violations in 27 states. Through this service, consumers are granted online access to view their doctor's professional background information (Wolfe, Kahn, & Resnevic, 2010). The NPDB is another official source of information on physician misconduct. Created by Congress in 1986 as part of the Health Care Quality Improvement Act, a host of agencies,[3] including SMBs, can report "adverse actions" by doctors and numerous other health care professionals (U.S. HHS, 2019, n.p.). At the national level, the NPDB has two primary goals. For one, improve cross-state information sharing regarding the quality of health care services delivered by providers. And two, prevent physicians with a history of misconduct or substandard care from quietly traversing across states. Despite the noble motivations behind this data collection initiative, all information contained in the NPDB is confidential, leaving the public with access to only a de-identified data file. Unfortunately, because physician identities are protected, the data, though informative, restricts the ability of patients to screen out potentially problematic physicians. Furthermore, an AJC investigative report into sexual misconduct pointed out multiple reasons why the NPDB is flawed. The noted shortcomings include evidence of private agreements between physicians and hospitals and legal loopholes that allow predatory doctors to escape the stigma of sexual misconduct (Ernsthausen, 2016). The report also highlighted large discrepancies between the number of sexual abuse cases reported in board orders, court records, and the news compared to the public use NPDB data. In fact, the report indicated that there were roughly 70% more physicians accused of sexual misconduct in other sources than indicated in the NPDB data (Ernsthausen, 2016).

A Challenging Endeavor

Despite the impressive lineup of laws, regulations, and acronyms, securing convictions of deviant physicians is a difficult task. Investigating and prosecuting these cases present several inherent challenges. First, given the scope and breadth of the medical services administered across the country, detecting fraud is not easy. As disclosed by former CMS Director of State Operations, Cindy Mann, the full extent of health care corruption evades us (Wright, 2009). With well over one billion fee-for-service claims and payments processed annually, unless obviously questionable billing patterns emerge, many crimes go unnoticed (Leap, 2011).

Beyond the challenges flowing from the complexity of these cases and the health care system, another difficulty in prosecuting health care fraud cases is proving that a crime occurred. For an act to be considered criminal, both *actus rea* "guilty act" and *mens rea* "guilty mind" must be present. However, the subjective nature of medical decision-making, in tandem with the expertise necessary to critique the judgments of physicians, further complicates arguments of criminal liability in cases of fraud and unnecessary surgery. Clinical decisions, for instance, are generally based on medical necessity. The problem that arises is that clinical disagreement is often the norm among medical experts, making these cases among the most difficult to prosecute (Buck, 2016). Case in point, in *United States v. Rutgard* (1997), two expert government witnesses, who were also ophthalmologists, disagreed over the medical necessity of several patients' cataract surgeries performed by the defendant. Whereas one expert testified that the operations adhered to the American Academy of Ophthalmology guidelines, the other believed that some of their conditions could have been treated without surgery (e.g., eyeglasses). In the end, several of the defendant's charges were dropped.

Even when prosecutors can establish evidence of wrongdoing that is just one side of the coin. On the other side, legal inquiries into FCA, AKS, and Stark Law violations, for example, require proof of the defendants' intent to "knowingly and willfully" commit fraud (Krause, 2006). Consider the recent case involving a Virginia dermatologist. According to a federal indictment, this doctor billed Medicare, Tricare, and other insurance companies for Mohs surgery and complex wound repairs that were deemed medically unnecessary. Allegedly, the defendant had deliberately misdiagnosed benign lesions as cancerous, forcing patients to undergo unnecessary surgery. With at least one medical expert agreeing with just about all of his diagnoses, reasonable doubt was cast on his intent to defraud, resulting in his acquittal on all 41 charges (Heim, 2015). This verdict not only underscores the difficulty of establishing intent but also demonstrates the complicated and subjective nature of medical decision-making.

Proving criminal intent can be vexing to prosecutors. For this reason, prosecutors may prefer pursuing facilitative crimes or offenses that support or enable health care crime (Bucy, 1989; TRAC, 2011). These crimes are much easier to prove and are often accompanied by lengthy sentences (Kyriakakis, 2015). Facilitative or auxiliary crimes include money laundering, mail and wire fraud, conspiracy, tax evasion, and obstruction of justice (Leap, 2011). In other instances, given the lower standard of proof required, prosecutors either singly or in conjunction with criminal proceedings, file civil rather than criminal charges against an alleged fraudster.

Sexual misconduct cases bring up similar concerns when examining the criminal justice response to deviant physicians; yet, some unique considerations also arise. More broadly, the criminal justice system has been criticized for not only responding inadequately to sexual violence, but for shifting focus to the victim's behavior rather than the offender's culpability as well. Cases involving physician offenders are no exception to this larger trend. In these cases, prosecutors face special challenges. Specifically, medical professionals may use their expertise to discount or explain away the experiences of the victim. In cases of improper touching (such as groping), for instance, a doctor may claim that it was part of an exam. Given the widespread inclination to blindly trust a trained doctor's professional opinion, authorities often take the physician's word for it. Even when there is clear evidence of misconduct, the criminal justice response may be insufficient. A 2015 case in California clearly demonstrates the leniency afforded to physicians in cases of sexual misbehavior. In this trial, a doctor faced charges for the alleged sexual victimization of six male patients at a clinic, with one accusation concerning the penetration of an unconscious victim with a foreign object. The physician pled no contest to five felony counts of sexual misconduct, but the judge did not send him to prison nor was he ordered to register as a sex offender. The judge's reasoning was based on evidence that a medication the defendant was taking reduced his ability to control his impulses, which, in turn, led to his hypersexual behavior (Wen, 2015). Instead, he received a five-year probation sentence. After one of his victims committed suicide, allegedly in response to the abuse, the bereaved family filed a law suit against him.

The Forgotten Victims

A longstanding indictment of the criminal justice process has been its treatment of victims. Health care fraud and abuse cases are no exception. Although the brunt of health care crime's physical toll usually falls squarely on the shoulders of aggrieved patients, the criminal justice system regularly fails to recognize the diverse harms experienced by individual victims. Even though the state serves as plaintiff for classic, *mala in se* crimes such as murder, rape, or robbery, punishments are closely tied to the pain caused to the actual victims. This is often not the case for victims of medical misconduct, who are usually relegated to the periphery. Most federal health care fraud indictments instead extensively describe the crimes against entities like Medicare, with little mention of victims. Our criminal justice system often transforms, as Kyriakakis (2015, p. 607) puts it, "a tale of unthinkable betrayal and patient abuse into something that looked more like an accounting scandal."

This focus on public and private insurers does not flow from nefarious intentions, however. Rather, legal structures, sentencing guidelines, internal incentives, bureaucratic pressures, and other political forces draw prosecutors' attention to "career-making" cases or those involving big dollar amounts (Bibas, 2012; Kyriakakis, 2015). Moreover, because the courts cannot possibly identify all the harms and victims of health care crimes, they tend to zero in on the monetary losses. Adding to this, the government has a clear financial interest in these cases. That is, if the government can successfully prove that a crime was committed by fraud or deceit, then the Mandatory Victim Restitution Act of 1996 (MVRA) mandates restitution in those amounts. In this way, the government can recover lost monies. Sadly, this often occurs at the expense of the victimized persons who are left to pick up the pieces.

Despite the failings of the justice system, the law provides other means for redressing patient injury. One path toward recourse for victims of deceptive and abusive clinicians is through medical malpractice lawsuits. Medical malpractice can take many forms. Among other inappropriate acts, failure to diagnose or misdiagnosis, misinterpreting or ignoring laboratory results, unnecessary surgery and treatments, wrong medication or dosage, and failure to order correct testing qualify as a violation of professional standards. While many of these acts mirror some of the deviant behaviors described throughout the text, criminal intent is not important here. Whether planned or not, if a claimant can prove that s/he was harmed in some way (e.g., medical costs, lost wages, pain and emotional suffering, and permanent and temporary disability and disfigurement), aggrieved parties could be compensated for damages. Importantly, however, while malpractice claims are commonplace (Jena, Seabury, Lakdawalla, & Chandra, 2011), nearly three-quarters of these cases end with claimants returning home empty-handed (Cohen & Hughes, 2007; Jena et al., 2011).

Conclusion

While most health care providers, physicians included, serve the public with integrity, a fair amount deal in the currency of deceit and corruption. The cost of health care crimes imposed on society is staggering, with public insurers and victimized patients often bearing the brunt of them. As presented in this chapter, several statutory and regulatory initiatives have been implemented by both state and federal governments to thwart fraud and sexual/physical abuse in the medical sector. These crime control and quality assurance efforts have led to the apprehension of numerous deviant physicians. Entities charged with curbing self-serving activities among health care professionals, however, encounter several challenges, perhaps the greatest of which involves establishing proof that an offense occurred. When these bad doctors are successfully prosecuted, punishment usually comes in the form of imprisonment, community supervision, and hefty fines. Restitution generally is paid to public insurers, not aggrieved patients, given the large sums of money lost by government-run public health care programs. Nonetheless, civil recourse is available for wronged patients through malpractice lawsuits but winning one of these cases is hard to come by. On this front, it is apparent that much more needs to be done to provide victims with a sense of justice.

Notes

1. Congress passed the Ethics in Patient Referral Act or Stark law in 1989 to address physician self-referrals. Penalties for Stark law violations include fines and exclusion from federal health care programs (for a comprehensive review of Stark law, see Sutton, 2011).
2. Importantly, no major healthcare-related legislation has been passed since President Obama left office in 2017. With the Trump administration shifting the focus of federal prosecutions away from corporations and toward individuals, it is unclear whether comprehensive health care reform remains a top cabinet-level priority (Swann, 2017).
3. Other authorized entities include, but are not limited to, medical malpractice payers, hospitals, professional societies, state law enforcement agencies, and HHS Office of the Inspector General.

References

AbuDagga, A., Wolfe, S. M., Carome, M., & Oshel, R. E. (2016). Cross-sectional analysis of the 1039 US physicians reported to the National Practitioner Data Bank for sexual misconduct, 2003–2013. *PLoS One*, *11*(2), 1–13.

Agency for Healthcare Administration. (2016). *The state's efforts to control Medicaid fraud and abuse*. Retrieved from http://ahca.myflorida.com/MCHQ/MPI/docs/Medicaid_Fraud_Abuse_Annual_Reports/2015-16_MedicaidFraudand AbuseAnnualReport.pdf

Anti-Kickback Statute, 42 USC. § 1320 (1972).

Bibas, S. (2012). *The machinery of criminal justice*. New York, NY: Oxford University Press.

Blank, S. M., Kasprisin, J. A., & White, A. C. (2009). Health care fraud. *American Criminal Law Review*, *46*(2), 701–759.

Buck, I. D. (2016). Overtreatment and informed consent: A fraud-based solution to unwanted and unnecessary care. *Florida State University Law Review*, *43*(3), 901–950.

Bucy, P. H. (1989). Fraud by fright: White collar crime by health care providers. *North Carolina Law Review*, *67*(4), 855–937.

Carr, G. D. (2003). Professional sexual misconduct: An overview. *Journal of the Mississippi State Medical Association*, *44*(9), 283–300.

Centers for Medicare and Medicaid Services. (2017). *The health care fraud and abuse control program protects consumers and taxpayers by combating health care fraud.* Retrieved from www.cms.gov/newsroom/fact-sheets/health-care-fraud-and-abuse-control-program-protects-consumers-and-taxpayers-combating-health-care-0

Civil False Claims Act, 31 USC. § 3729 (1863).

Cohen, T. H., & Hughes, K. A. (2007). *Medical malpractice insurance claims in seven states, 2000–2004.* Washington, DC: U.S. Department of Justice.

Department of Justice. (2018a). *Dallas physicians and nurses sentenced to prison for role in $11 million Medicare fraud scheme.* Retrieved from www.justice.gov/opa/pr/dallas-physicians-and-nurses-sentenced-prison-role-11-million-medicare-fraud-scheme

Department of Justice. (2018b). *Detroit clinic owner sentenced to over 13 years in prison for $8.9 million health care fraud scheme.* Retrieved from www.justice.gov/opa/pr/detroit-clinic-owner-sentenced-over-13-years-prison-89-million-health-care-fraud-scheme

Department of Justice. (2018c). *Doctor sentenced to two years in prison for taking bribes in test-referral scheme with New Jersey clinical lab.* Retrieved from www.justice.gov/usao-nj/pr/doctor-sentenced-two-years-prison-taking-bribes-test-referral-scheme-new-jersey-clinical

Department of Justice. (2018d). *Strike force operations.* Retrieved from www.justice.gov/criminal-fraud/strike-force-operations

Eisler, P., & Hansen, B. (2013, August 20). Thousands of doctors practicing despite errors, misconduct. *USA Today.* Retrieved from www.usatoday.com/story/news/nation/2013/08/20/doctors-licenses-medical-boards/2655513/

Ernsthausen, J. (2016, July). Dangerous doctors, flawed data: Why a national tracking system doesn't show the extent of physician sexual misconduct. *The Atlanta Journal Constitution.* Retrieved from http://doctors.ajc.com/sex_abuse_national_database/

Fauber, J., & Wynn, M. (2018, November 30). 7 takeaways from our year-long investigation into the country's broken medical license system. *USA Today.* Retrieved from www.usatoday.com/story/news/2018/11/30/medical-board-license-discipline-failures-7-takeaways-investigation/2092321002/

Federation of State Medical Boards. (2019). *US medical regulatory trends and actions.* Retrieved from www.fsmb.org/siteassets/advocacy/publications/us-medical-regulatory-trends-actions.pdf

Gable, L. (2011). The Patient Protection and Affordable Care Act, public health, and the elusive target of human rights. *The Journal of Law, Medicine & Ethics, 39*(3), 340–354.

Garner, C. B., & McCabe, D. (2012). The evolving relationships between hospital, physician and patient in modern American healthcare. *Health, Culture and Society, 3*(1), 150–158.

Grant, D., & Alfred, K. C. (2007). Sanctions and recidivism: An evaluation of physician discipline by state medical boards. *Journal of Health Politics, Policy and Law, 32*(5), 867–885.

Health Insurance Portability and Accountability Act, Pub. L. No. 104–191, 110 Stat. 1936 (1996).

Heim, J. (2015, November 30). Northern Va. dermatologist acquitted on charges of insurance fraud. *The Washington Post*. Retrieved from www.washingtonpost. com/local/northern-virginia-dermatologist-acquitted-on-charges-of-insurance-fraud/2015/11/30/405c1bec-7e82-11e5-b575-d8dcfedb4ea1_story.html?utm_term=.b45bdfbfcd0a

Jena, A. B., Seabury, S., Lakdawalla, D., & Chandra, A. (2011). Malpractice risk according to physician specialty. *New England Journal of Medicine, 365*(7), 629–636.

Johnson, D. A., & Chaudhry, H. J. (2012). *Medical licensing and discipline in America: A history of the Federation of State Medical Boards*. Lanham, MD: Lexington Books.

Krause, J. H. (2006). Fraud in universal coverage: The usual suspects (and then some). *Kansas Law Review, 55*, 1151.

Kyriakakis, A. (2015). The missing victims of health care fraud. *Utah Law Review, 2015*(3), 605–657.

Leap, T. L. (2011). *Phantom billing, fake prescriptions, and the high cost of medicine*. Ithaca, NY: Cornell University Press.

Leape, L. L. (1992). Unnecessary surgery. *Annual Review of Public Health, 13*(1), 363–383.

Mannava, K. A., Bercovitch, L., & Grant-Kels, J. M. (2013). Kickbacks, stark violations, client billing, and joint ventures: Facts and controversies. *Clinics in Dermatology, 31*(6), 764–768.

McPeak, J. M. (2018). *Rising health care costs: Drivers, challenges and solutions*. Retrieved from www.naic.org/documents/cipr_study_1812_health_care_costs.pdf

Morris, L. (2009). Combating fraud in health care: An essential component of any cost containment strategy. *Health Affairs, 28*(5), 1351–1356.

Morrison, A. W. (2000). An analysis of anti-kickback and self-referral law in modern health care. *Journal of Legal Medicine, 21*(3), 351–394.

New York State Attorney General's Office. (2019). *A. G. Schneiderman announces sentencing of pharmacist in connection with $150 million Medicaid fraud scam*. Retrieved from https://ag.ny.gov/press-release/ag-schneiderman-announces-sentencing-pharmacist-connection-150-million-medicaid-fraud

Nokes, S. S. (2016). Medicaid, the MFCU, and you. *US Attorney's Bulletin, 64*, 69–72.

Office of the Inspector General. (2017). *A roadmap for new physicians: Avoiding Medicare and Medicaid fruad and abuse*. Retrieved from https://oig.hhs.gov/compliance/physician-education/roadmap_web_version.pdf

Papanicolas, I., Woskie, L. R., & Jha, A. K. (2018). Health care spending in the United States and other high-income countries. *JAMA, 319*(10), 1024–1039.

Patient Protection and Affordable Care Act, 42 USC. § 300 (2010).

Pontell, H. N., Jesilow, P. D., & Geis, G. (1982). Policing physicians: Practitioner fraud and abuse in a government medical program. *Social Problems, 30*(1), 117–125.

Roy, A. (2011). Saving Medicare from itself. *National Affairs, 8*(11), 35–55.

Sparrow, M. K. (2008). Fraud in the US health-care system: Exposing the vulnerabilities of automated payments systems. *Social Research: An International Quarterly, 75*(4), 1151–1180.

Sullivan, J. (2018). *Proactive planning for HHS-OIG-DOJ investigations*. Retrieved from www.policymed.com/2013/05/proactive-planning-for-hhs-oig-doj-investigations.html

Sutton, P. A. (2011). The Stark law in retrospect. *Annals of Health Law, 20*(1), 15–48.

Swann, J. (2017, May 25). Trump budget would boost health-care fraud-fighting efforts. *Bloomberg BNA*. Retrieved from www.bna.com/trump-budget-boost-b73014451549/

Teegardin, C., Robbins, D., Ernsthausen, J., & Hart, A. (2016). *License to betray: A broken system forgives doctors in every state.* Retrieved from http://doctors.ajc.com/doctors_sex_abuse/

Transactional Records Access Clearinghouse (TRAC). (2011). *Health care fraud prosecutions for 2011.* Retrieved from https://trac.syr.edu/tracreports/crim/258/

United States v. Rutgard, 116 F.3d 1270 (1997).

U.S. Department of Health and Human Services. (2018a). *Health care fraud and abuse control program annual report for fiscal year 2017.* Retrieved from https://oig.hhs.gov/publications/docs/hcfac/FY2017-hcfac.pdf

U.S. Department of Health and Human Services. (2018b). *Medicaid fraud control units fiscal year 2017 annual report.* Retrieved from https://oig.hhs.gov/oei/reports/oei-09-18-00180.pdf

U.S. Department of Health and Human Services. (2019). *What is the NPDB?* Retrieved from www.npdb.hrsa.gov/resources/whatIsTheNPDB.jsp

Wen, M. (2015, April 19). Former Tang Center doctor sentenced to 5 years' probation for sexual misconduct with patients. *The Daily Californian*. Retrieved from www.dailycal.org/2015/04/18/former-tang-center-doctor-sentenced-to-5-years-probation-for-sexual-misconduct-with-patients/

Wolfe, S. M., Kahn, R., & Resnevic, K. (2010). *Public Citizen's Health Research Group ranking of the rate of state medical boards' serious disciplinary actions, 2007–2009.* Retrieved from www.citizen.org/hrg1905

Wright, S. (2009). *SIS data usefulness for detecting fraud, waste, and abuse.* Retrieved from https://oig.hhs.gov/oei/reports/oei-04-07-00240.pdf

5 Concluding Remarks

Similar to the findings of criminologists, a review of the existing literature suggests that the vast majority of doctors are ethical, law-abiding professionals while a small number of physicians are responsible for the vast majority of deviant behavior (National Health Care Anti-Fraud Association, 2019). This small group of deviant doctors, however, have a major impact on individual victims, the medical profession, and society. In this concluding chapter, we aim to highlight the contribution of criminological perspectives in understanding deviance within the practice of medicine. Within this discussion, we outline several policy recommendations, as well as directions for future scholarly research that may assist in efforts to prevent and/or reduce misconduct by doctors.

Criminological Insight Into Physician Deviance

The amount of power and trust allocated to physicians within the context of the complex American health care system, which is characterized by a lack of meaningful oversight mechanisms, culminates in an environment ripe for fraud and abuse. Despite the plethora of initiatives at the state and national level aimed at medical fraud and abuse, persistent waste and violence continue at varying degrees across the country. Throughout this text, references have been made to ethical guidelines and mantras relevant to physicians, including the well-known Hippocratic Oath and the AMA's code of ethics. The cases of fraud and abuse referenced in the media and research illustrate a clear disconnect between the various professional codes of conduct supported by professional organizations and the actual behavior of physicians practicing in the field. We have sought to explain professional misconduct and illegal behavior by applying criminological perspectives to this form of deviance. These perspectives provide key insight into why doctors who are charged with protecting the interests of their patients may violate this trust for their own personal gain, whether it be financially motivated or for personal gratification. Drawing upon the field of criminology, there are multiple potential avenues for addressing physician deviance. The discussion that follows will draw upon elements from routine activities, deterrence, neutralization, and control balance theory to tackle different aspects of this complex social problem. Although these perspectives often vary in focus and underlying assumptions about criminal behavior, the recommendations drawn from each often overlap.

Within a routine activities theoretical framework, it is assumed that motivated offenders will always exist, and rather than addressing offenders, avenues for crime prevention/reduction should focus on target hardening (Cohen & Felson, 1979). The objective of target hardening techniques is to reduce target suitability and increase capable guardianship. Accordingly, misconduct could be reduced by empowering patients with information to assist in the selection of trustworthy doctors and to be assertive in their decisions relevant to their personal health care. It is also imperative that other individuals and entities responsible for providing guardianship, such as other medical staff and medical boards, fulfill their obligations of attending to patient care and well-being. The following measures may assist in improving guardianship and reducing the attractiveness of patients as victims:

- Enhanced public access to annual, nationwide medical figures, data, and reports to assist in patient decision-making.
- Public disclosure of offending physician identities and case details in the NPDB.
- Educational campaigns aimed at raising public awareness about proper patient-physician relationships and boundaries, as well as outline what is proper and improper behavior during medical exams.
- The use of guardians in exam rooms whether it is a trusted outside party (i.e., patient's family member or friend) or the mandated presence of a nurse/other medical staff during physical exams.
- Mechanisms in place for the protection of "whistle-blowers" in the medical community such as nurses and other medical staff who may disclose physician deviance—these individuals may fail to report if they fear losing their jobs or anticipate being blacklisted in the medical community for reporting.
- Concerted efforts to encourage reports of misbehavior to legal authorities such as the police—this could be accomplished through public awareness campaigns and flyers in medical offices.

In comparison to routine activities, deterrence theory centers on the offender's rationality and ability to weight costs and benefits of crime. Thus, from this perspective, a way to reduce physician misconduct would be the implementation of greater consequences for misbehavior. As previously discussed in *Chapter 3*, for an offender to be deterred, the consequences for crime/deviance must be swift, certain, and severe. The current structure of the American health care system and associated practices affect the overall deterrent effect of potential sanctions. For instance, the FFS model and medical record-keeping practices hinder detection of fraudulent practices, while a lack of strong institutional and weak criminal justice response to abuse by doctors diminishes the certainty and severity of existing sanctions. Also related to the offender decision-making process, neutralization and control balance theory emphasize the processes that underlie the improper exercise of power across situations. To briefly review, neutralization theory suggests that offenders suppress their conventional beliefs, like adherence to formal ethical codes and standards for care, by employing cognitive restructuring mechanisms to eliminate cognitive dissonance when their behavior does not match espoused beliefs. In comparison, control balance theory suggests doctors may be inclined to offend when they have an excess of power in a current situation compared to the level of control they are subjected to. The following recommendations could aid in striking a stronger imbalance in the perception of costs over benefit in the commission of fraud and abuse, while simultaneously influencing the amount of power physicians are subjected to in a given situation. Moreover, the subsequent measures may affect physicians' application of neutralization techniques to absolve their bonds to professional codes of ethics:

- Greater transparency in medical record keeping and sharing—the increased accountability provided in this regard serves as a deterrent to the falsification of patient records.
- The implementation of a checks and balances system, one in which all *medical equipment* orders are cross-referenced for verification of cost-efficiency, accuracy, and justification of allotted purchases.
- The regulation of FFS costs through the integration of a standard, predetermined, fixed payment system for all patient-related services.
- A comprehensive verification system hierarchically identifying necessary versus unnecessary surgeries.
- Stiffer criminal penalties for doctors who sexually abuse patients.
- Mandatory disclosure of physician misconduct by hospitals and medical practices accompanied by regulations to preclude facilities from circumventing such disclosures through legal or policy loopholes (i.e., non-disclosure agreements and policies that permit for the physician to resign rather than face termination).
- More emphasis on ethical conduct and behavior during medical training and improved continuing education efforts once doctors enter medical practice.

- Enhanced professional sanctions for misbehavior that are actually applied to offending physicians rather than rules that act as mere "guidelines" for behavior and result in few sanctions being imposed in reality.

Acknowledging the immense task of responding to physician deviance, the aforementioned policy recommendations only scratch the surface. It is vital to recognize that many of these changes would require a major overhaul to parts of the U.S. health care system that may not even be feasible at this point such as changing the fee-for-service structure. A more modest first step lies in what is apparent upon a review of the extant literature. More research is needed in the area of physician deviance. Especially when considering the disciplines of criminal justice and criminology, our knowledge about victims of physician misconduct and this class of offenders is markedly lacking. While studies of this behavior and its effects are characterized by challenges (e.g., social desirability bias and identifying appropriate populations to draw samples), scholars must begin to mount barriers and endeavor to collect data about crime and deviance in the medical field. Additional qualitative studies based on snow-ball samples of victims and offenders may be the key to developing more nuanced measures that can be piloted in larger scale, quantitative studies. Valid self-report measures of victimization and offending in the context of medicine must be developed and creative methodologies need to be employed to garner the information needed to more accurately quantify the extent and nature of physician deviance.

References

Cohen, L. E., & Felson, M. (1979). Social change and crime rate trends: A routine activity approach. *American Sociological Review, 44*(4), 588–608.

National Health Care Anti-Fraud Association. (2019). *The challenge of health care fraud*. Washington, DC: NHCAA. Retrieved from www.nhcaa.org/resources/health-care-anti-fraud-resources/the-challenge-of-health-care-fraud.aspx

Index

Note: Page numbers in *italics* indicate figures.

Taylor & Francis eBooks

www.taylorfrancis.com

A single destination for eBooks from Taylor & Francis
with increased functionality and an improved user
experience to meet the needs of our customers.

90,000+ eBooks of award-winning academic content in
Humanities, Social Science, Science, Technology, Engineering,
and Medical written by a global network of editors and authors.

TAYLOR & FRANCIS EBOOKS OFFERS:

A streamlined
experience for
our library
customers

A single point
of discovery
for all of our
eBook content

Improved
search and
discovery of
content at both
book and
chapter level

REQUEST A FREE TRIAL
support@taylorfrancis.com

 Routledge
Taylor & Francis Group

 CRC Press
Taylor & Francis Group